The Times and Trials
of Anne Hutchinson

LANDMARK LAW CASES

AMERICAN SOCIETY

Peter Charles Hoffer
N. E. H. Hull
Series Editors

MICHAEL P. WINSHIP

The Times and Trials of Anne Hutchinson

Puritans Divided

UNIVERSITY PRESS OF KANSAS

Published by the University Press of Kansas (Lawrence, Kansas 66049), which was organized by the Kansas Board of Regents and is operated and funded by Emporia State University, Fort Hays State University, Kansas State University, Pittsburg State University, the University of Kansas, and Wichita State University

Library of Congress Cataloging-in-Publication Data

Winship, Michael P. (Michael Paul)
The times and trials of Anne Hutchinson : Puritans divided / Michael P. Winship.
p.   cm — (Landmark law cases & American society)
Includes bibliographical references and index.
ISBN 0-7006-1379-x (cloth : alk. paper) — ISBN 0-7006-1380-3 (pbk. : alk. paper)
1. Puritans — Massachusetts — History — 17th century.   2. Congregational churches — Massachusetts — History — 17th century.   3. Hutchinson, Anne (Marbury) 1591–1643.   4. Antinomianism.   5. Massachusetts — Church history — 17th century.   6. Massachusetts — Religious life and customs.
7. Massachusetts — History — Colonial period, ca. 1600–1775.
I. Title.   II. Series.
BX7148.M4W55 2005
273'.6'09744 — dc22   2004025495

British Library Cataloguing-in-Publication Data is available.

Printed in the United States of America

10 9 8 7 6 5 4 3 2 1

For Michael McGiffert

CONTENTS

One might wonder why the nearly four-hundred-year-old civil and church trials of Anne Hutchinson for contempt and doctrinal error would continue to command so much scholarly attention today. She was no Joan of Arc, leading her knights against the invader and burned at the stake for heresy, nor a Mary, Queen of Scots, reaching for the English throne and executed for treason. She was a mother, wife, and congregant exiled from Massachusetts Bay Colony for refusing to truckle to authority. The offenses were comparatively minor ones (though they led to her banishment and excommunication), yet the trials still have the power to grip our imagination and, after all that has been written of them, still demand a full accounting.

In 1941, L. Adamson Hoebel, an anthropologist, and Karl N. Llewellyn, a law professor, published a study of Cheyenne Indian law ways. They proposed that certain "cases of trouble" opened a window into lost worlds of law, society, and culture. While Hutchinson's was not the first trial sowing dissension in the puritan commonwealth of Massachusetts Bay (in fact, it was preceded by the trials of Roger Williams and came near the end of a series of conflicts called the free grace or antinomian controversy), it revealed overlapping, inherent tensions in the new colony, its puritan way, and its forms for self-government.

Michael Winship's wise and learned study of the times and trials of Anne Hutchinson is in a sense a study of the founding of America. In it, we rediscover how rooted our history is in transatlantic religious chronicle. In Hutchinson's time, Massachusetts Bay was a lonely and distant outpost of an English commercial empire in the making, but for Hutchinson and the other characters in her story, the colony was much more that a mart for timber, fish, and furs. It was a place where the pious might gather to explore and exult their salvation, far from the intrusive eyes of English religious and political authorities.

Today, it is not fashionable to speak of the puritan origins of American ideas, but Winship's remarkably concise retelling of the times and trials moves puritan doctrine and worship back into focus. The congeries of villages of farmers, fishermen, craftsmen, merchants, servants, laborers, mothers, fathers, and children that constituted the colony resembled a composite of England's towns and countryside, with one notable difference — there was no place in England, or all the world for that matter, more literate or more convinced of its central part in God's plan for the world. Out of the colony's contentions would spring, in the fullness of time, forms of American democracy, our sense of mission, our entrepreneurship, and our belief in the rule of law.

Historians have examined these beginnings and applied them retroactively to the tumults of Hutchinson's brief stay in the colony. Thus her trials became, for different historians, a test of women's rights; the combat of mysticism and revelation versus worldliness and pragmatism; a contest over who would rule in the colony; a part of the story of a rising merchant cadre; and a moment in the struggle for freedom of speech and worship, among others. As Winship demonstrates, it was not really any of these for the people who lived it.

Instead, seeing the crisis as they did, he recenters it in a world of theological contentions. For puritans not only acted in pious ways and sought salvation but also endlessly reexamined the meaning of piety and salvation. The trials began with one such quarrel between two brilliant ministers as different in personality and, within puritanism, in theology, as they could be. He lets these protagonists speak for themselves, and he takes them at their word. At the same time, he translates their complex, rich and arcane points of contention for us. Into their dispute entered leading magistrates, for they not only demanded good order and respect for the ministry but were personally interested in the outcome of the dispute. Members of the ministers' congregations, including Anne Hutchinson, had parts to play as well, and as the crisis neared its climax, her role grew paramount.

Winship's account blends dramatic vigor with intellectual veracity in a fashion that will make it a benchmark for all others. It is controversial in the best sense, supplanting its predecessors while providing fuel for a new round of assessments in the years to come. So long as governments take it upon themselves to define orthodoxies of conscience, whether by arbitrary imposition under the trappings of law or by denying legal redress to those whose opinions it condemns, *The Times and Trials of Anne Hutchinson* will be required reading. Indeed, Winship's discussion of religious intolerance and immoderation could not be more timely than it is today.

ACKNOWLEDGMENTS

Peter Hoffer, Eleanor Winship, and Michael Zuckerman read and commented on the manuscript, to its great benefit. Peter Hoffer roped me into the project in the first place and kept it from collapsing. It seemed especially appropriate to dedicate this book to a person who has put a great deal of effort over the years into getting me to make my ideas about puritanism both coherent and readable. My thanks to them all.

Substantial sections of the book are adapted from my *Making Heretics: Militant Protestantism and Free Grace in Massachusetts, 1636–1641* (Princeton, N.J.: Princeton University Press, 2002). I thank Princeton University Press for giving me permission to use this material.

The seventeenth-century English spelling and grammar in the quotations have been occasionally revised for easier comprehension. Bible quotations are from the King James version.

Anne Hutchinson was a prophet, spiritual adviser, mother of fifteen, and important participant in a fierce religious controversy that shook the infant Massachusetts Bay Colony from 1636 to 1638. Everyone agreed that the free grace of God converted and saved sinners. But how? Did it transform them? Overwhelm them? Leave its traces mainly in signs of holiness or mainly in rushing joy? And if people disagreed with you on this issue, were they agents of Satan attempting to destroy the colony? The controversy pushed Massachusetts to the brink of collapse and spurred a significant exodus. English publishers eagerly printed and reprinted the sermons it generated, and one particularly fiery collection has been reprinted steadily down to today. As the controversy wound down, the government tried Hutchinson for slandering the colony's ministers, blamed the entire dispute on her, and sentenced her to banishment. Soon thereafter, the Boston church, to which she belonged, tried her for heresy and excommunicated her for lying. Hutchinson's well-publicized trials and the attendant accusations against her made her the most famous, or infamous, Englishwoman in colonial American history.

So much sound and fury might seem surprising from such a tiny colony. From its founding in 1630, Massachusetts had grown to only about eight thousand English people by 1638. Far more English immigrants went to the West Indies and the Chesapeake in the 1630s. But size was not the measure of Massachusetts's importance. The colony's founders were puritans, militant Protestants who sought to reform their country's only legal church, the Church of England. They, and Hutchinson herself, left England because their religious and political ambitions clashed with those of King Charles I. The immigrants' English allies kept a close eye on Massachusetts, hoping that it would succeed in setting up a much holier society than England's and worrying that it would descend into an extremism that would discredit all puritans. King Charles's councillors, on the other hand, feared the colony's capacity to foster resistance to his government. They periodically set up loyalty tests for would-be immigrants, and they spent most of the 1630s trying to get the colony's royal charter, its legal basis, quashed in English courts.

Hutchinson's story is superficially a familiar one, having been told and retold many times over the last three and a half centuries. This book is based on the most extensive research into the controversy around her to date. As archives were combed for neglected manuscripts and obscure three-hundred-year-old books perused for scattered references, that story took on an unfamiliar shape. The three conventionally important characters remained: Hutchinson herself; John Winthrop, the often reelected governor of Massachusetts, more tolerant than many of his fellows, but prepared to repress hard when he felt it was called for; and John Cotton, a famous minister, mild and nonconfrontational, but with distinctly odd theological ideas.

Joining them, however, were people whose significance had not yet been understood. The minister Thomas Shepard, an angry militant heresy hunter, vigorously pursued both Cotton and Hutchinson. He kept the flames of controversy stoked high even as he claimed to be trying to quench them. Working along with him appeared other figures, less well documented but no less eager to purge the colony of people they considered deviants. Most notable of these was Thomas Dudley, who, next to Winthrop, was the most important leader in Massachusetts.

Two figures usually incorrectly presented as "followers" of Hutchinson began to take on important, independent roles of their own. Henry Vane, well connected at King Charles's court and governor of the colony from 1636 to 1637, had a prodigious appetite for unconventional speculation. Vane's enthusiastic participation in radical theology emboldened his supporters and terrified opponents like Shepard, who could not touch him because of his status. He was far more feared than Hutchinson, for the good reason that he could do far more damage to the colony. John Wheelwright, a bellicose minister and Anne Hutchinson's brother-in-law, was a lightning rod for the frustrations and anxieties of his fellow ministers. Vane, Wheelwright, and Hutchinson drew support and allies from a coalition of now-shadowy but determined and creative activists.

This expanded group of players requires an expanded context for Hutchinson's trials. Most accounts of Hutchinson pay little attention to the year between her alleged crime of slander and the trial for it in November 1637 that got her banished. Yet that year saw a convulsive political struggle — triggered by the controversial trial of Wheelwright in March 1637—that almost destroyed the colony. Vane, Wheelwright's staunch supporter, left four months later. Only after Vane's departure did a measure of stability return to the colony, allowing Hutchinson and a number of others to be tried. Hutchinson's trials must be placed in the context of the religious, political, and legal turmoil that had preceded and prompted them.

We tend to think of legal systems as secular. England, however, had many kinds of courts, including religious ones, and they dealt with many kinds of cases, civil, criminal, and spiritual. The puritans of Massachusetts set up a combined secular and religious legal system very different than England's. Through it, they tried to preserve a unified Christian society in accordance with what they understood to be God's will. God's will, they believed, required religious intolerance. Tolerance insulted God, risked people's souls, endangered the government, and broke down the community. The trials of Hutchinson and her allies were an attempt to use the law to protect the unity of Massachusetts's Christian society, but instead, they almost tore that society apart.

Concepts of law even affected religious issues being debated in this controversy. Salvation came when God as judge pronounced sinners free from the guilt of sin and from its punishment of damnation. That pronouncement was called justification. How people could know that God had justified them was one of the major questions of the dispute. Another issue was whether God's moral laws any longer had power over a person whom He had justified. People who answered no were denounced as heretical "antinomians." Nineteenth-century historians, in a mistaken belief that antinomianism was the central issue in the controversy, mislabeled it the "antinomian controversy." In fact, the term "antinomianism" was rarely applied by contemporaries, for good reason, as will be seen, although one would never guess that from reading most scholarly accounts of Hutchinson. The controversy will be referred to in this book as the free grace controversy, since all participants agreed that their dispute was about the nature of the grace that God freely bestowed on those whom He intended to save.

A trial can be a legal event, but more broadly, it means any kind of test, and puritans expected that God would be constantly trying them. He sent his trials to expose their weaknesses, demonstrate their faithfulness or lack of it, and display his glory. All the participants in the free grace controversy agreed that it was a divine trial. But whom God intended to try and for what purposes were hotly disputed questions.

—————

The free grace controversy was created and driven by extraordinary and often fearful stories that the settlers of Massachusetts told with increasing vehemence about themselves and their colony. Those stories reflected the turbulence and religious violence of the times in which they lived; stories of the coming end of the world; of Roman Catholic secret agents plotting to undermine the colony; of boatloads of heretics intending an invasion; of schemes to massacre the clergy; and, finally, as the crisis was winding down, a story of an "American Jezebel," a woman as wicked as the biblical queen of that name, raised up by Satan to overthrow the churches and the government of the colony.

That final story of Hutchinson has shaped subsequent accounts both of her and of the controversy in which she was enmeshed. But it was perhaps the most calculated of all the stories circulating in Massachusetts. There were powerful men whose messy roles needed to be covered up and a colony whose institutions had not performed brilliantly in this moment of great stress. Blaming Hutchinson for the entire controversy allowed much else to be swept under the rug.

The story also gave Hutchinson near-legendary status. As with all legends, what exactly she stood for has shifted over the centuries. Winthrop and his allies portrayed her as a hell-spawned agent of destructive anarchy. Nineteenth-century America celebrated the new achievement of separation of church and state, and it discovered in her a crusader for religious liberty. As the struggle for women's rights gathered steam in the twentieth century, she became a feminist leader, who terrified the patriarchs of Massachusetts not so much for the intricacies of what she believed in but because she was an assertive, highly visible woman. The relationship of what we know of the historical Hutchinson, insofar as she can be reconstructed, and the legendary Hutchinson is one topic of this book.

Hutchinson has kept her relevance in recent centuries because people have seen her as ahead of her time, as someone in opposition to the patriarchal, bigoted world of the seventeenth century. The historical Anne Hutchinson, however, fit fairly comfortably into that seemingly alien and claustrophobic world. Furthermore, that world itself is not necessarily as distant as some of those who write about Hutchinson believe or hope. As I write, the White House is occupied by a conservative Protestant (descended from Hutchinson) who believes that God placed him there and who is actively trying to break down long-established boundaries between religion and the state. Almost 30 percent of the American people anticipate the Second Coming of Jesus. The United States is engaged in what amounts to the most geographically widespread religious war in history. At least some of the leaders on the American side of that war see it as one in which the partisans of the true God are facing idol worshipers. A federal court has created a firestorm of almost universal protest for ordering the words "under God" taken out of the Pledge of Allegiance. Lawns in my southern town are currently dotted with small signs, protesting the forced removal of a Ten Commandments monument from the Alabama Supreme Court. Intolerance and the nature of the proper relationship between religion, the state, and individuals were the burning issues of Hutchinson's trials, and they are still very much with us today.

CHAPTER I

The Making of a Prophet

Anne Marbury Hutchinson was born in 1591 in the small market town of Alford, Lincolnshire, six miles from the North Sea and about 125 miles northeast of London. Queen Elizabeth had reigned for almost thirty-three years, in spite of numerous Catholic plots to overthrow her. England, Europe's most powerful Protestant country, had been continually engaged in inconclusive and expensive warfare against Catholic enemies since 1585. A gigantic storm and lethal fire boats saved England from the Catholic Spanish Armada in 1588. Nonetheless, a steady stream of Catholic priests continued to slip into the country, risking grisly execution in order to rouse England's remaining Catholics. English pirates and adventurers harassed and plundered Spain's New World empire, while English visionaries planned a great Protestant empire in North America. Shakespeare was writing his first plays, and William Byrd was composing the most sublime of all English music. The population of England continued to rise rapidly, in spite of devastating outbreaks of the plague and occasional famines. Work was in increasingly short supply, and the swelling numbers of vagrants terrified people who had property to protect. It was commonly accepted that the world was in the final days before Christ returned for the Last Judgment.

For the Marburys, England's most calamitous event of 1591 would have been the trials of important zealous Protestant friends and acquaintances in London. Being on the wrong side of the law, at least as Her Majesty's servants interpreted the law, was no new thing for them. Did Anne's father, Francis, tell her of the day in 1578 when he, a twenty-two-year-old clergyman, had been pulled from his prison to face a grilling from the bishop of London? His offense: the bishop of Peterborough had ordered him to leave the market town of Northampton, and he had defiantly returned to continue his denunciations of the Church of England, to which all of Queen Elizabeth's subjects were required to belong.

The bishop of London told Marbury that he was a puritan, or, more precisely, "an overthwart proud Puritan knave." The "puritan" part of the label at least fit, although Marbury, like most puritans, resented the term as an insult. Queen Elizabeth had finished the task of changing the Church of England from Roman Catholicism to Protestantism in 1559. But she was a religious conservative. Not all her subjects thought that she had gone far enough to cleanse the church of Catholic rites and government or to ensure that the church had ministers capable of saving souls by their powerful preaching. Those critics were called by their opponents "puritans." Moderate puritans were mainly concerned with spreading their severe moral code and providing zealous preachers in each of England's parishes. Less compromising puritans wanted to purge the Church of England of all the elements they regarded as sinful and nonbiblical — the church's official prayer book, its priestly garments, and kneeling at the Lord's Supper (Jesus' disciples sat when he gave them his last supper), among other offenses. In the meantime, they refused to conform to those elements.

Marbury was among the most radical of the nonconforming puritans, the presbyterians. They wanted to abolish all the pomp and ceremony of the Church of England and remodel its government according to what they thought was the Bible's simple, consensual pattern. Presbyterians would eliminate bishops, who were appointed by the monarch, and who in turn appointed each parish's minister and supervised its affairs. Instead, in the presbyterians' system, the sincere Christians in each parish would choose their church's "elders" or governors, consisting of two ministers (a teacher in charge of doctrine and a pastor in charge of people's souls) and a ruling lay elder (there were other less important officers). Those sincere Christians would participate in the sacraments, while they and the elders coerced and cajoled the rest of the parish to higher levels of godliness. Elders from many churches would meet in regional and national synods to supervise the conduct of individual churches. Government courts would work hand in hand with the elders of the parishes to stamp out immorality and heresies in England.

To bring about that renewed golden age of grassroots Christianity, presbyterians furiously denounced the bishops and the incompetent ministers the bishops appointed, which is what Marbury was doing with gusto before his interrogators. For every soul, Marbury warned the Bishop of London, whom your lack of good preachers damns, the guilt is on your hands. "Thou art a very ass, an idiot, and a fool," the bishop told Marbury. He ordered Marbury back to prison, and Marbury warned him to beware the judgments of God. Shortly thereafter, Marbury wrote down an account of his interrogation and circulated it, so that other puritans could tremble at the wickedness of bishops and draw courage from Marbury's defiance of them.

Marbury defied the bishops not in the name of religious liberty but in the name of God's truth. Even nonconforming puritans like Marbury did not believe in freedom of conscience — the most zealous puritans wanted to execute all the Catholics left in England, after giving them a period to convert. Religious liberty, to puritans, was the compulsory duty of a unified Christian community to obey God's will. In their own eyes, puritans were the most patriotic subjects of the monarch, since the most Protestant. Their opponents in the Church of England, however, deemed them disloyal to queen and church, and they did their best to suppress them.

Puritan agitation rose during the 1580s. Elizabeth thwarted parliamentary efforts in the middle years of that decade to reform the Church of England along puritan lines, while the most important puritan sympathizers among her councillors died. In desperation, presbyterians set up clandestine synods of their own. The government discovered them in 1589 and arrested the ringleaders. Their trials stretched out through 1591 and petered out inconclusively, but they broke the back of puritan agitation. One of the presbyterians' last gestures was to publish in the Netherlands *A Parte of a Register* in 1592. This collection of defiant puritan tracts against the bishops included Marbury's account of his interrogation. Anne was born during the death throes of the puritan effort to comprehensively fashion a biblically reformed society. That effort would be reborn almost forty years later with the migration to Massachusetts.

———

Both of Anne's parents belonged to the gentry, the small group of some ten thousand interrelated families who ruled England. Francis and his second wife, Bridget Dryden, came from families with coats of arms and had brothers who were knighted. Bridget's birthplace, Canons Ashby House, is a tourist attraction today. Her brother Sir Erasmus Dryden (grandfather to the famous poet John Dryden) was a leading protector of puritan ministers.

Puritans called the family a school for the church and common-wealth, and Francis and Bridget clearly did their pedagogical duty care-fully by Anne. As the patriarch of the family, Francis would have led the family every day in prayers, reading and exposition of the Bible, catechism drill, and psalm singing. Bridget trained Anne in the arts of nursing, supervising a household, and looking after a fast-increasing number of younger brothers and sisters. She was also probably the one who taught Anne how to read. Anne's formidable command of the Bible would have started with the memorization of scripture passages almost as soon as she could speak, and she might have started reading scripture not long afterward. Anne knew how to write, as well, a rare accomplishment among English women in general, although not unusual in the upper strata of society. On Sunday evenings, the family would have gathered to go over the sermons, up to two hours long, that they had heard earlier that day in church. Francis would have probed Anne on what she remembered; some godly girls were taking notes at sermons before they were six. Conventicles (private religious gatherings) with like-minded friends would also have been part of the family routine. Anne would have been encouraged to develop her own regular private habits of prayer and meditation.

In the first decade of Anne's life, she might have heard talk among the adults about how England's religious situation would soon change. Elderly, unmarried Queen Elizabeth could not live much longer (although any speculation about the queen's death had to be done very quietly because it was a crime). Scotland was presbyterian, and its king, James VI, was to assume the English throne.

But while Elizabeth held on to life in the 1590s, James engaged in protracted political battles with the Scottish presbyterians. From those battles, he concluded that presbyterianism was too democratic for kings. The more authoritarian, Crown-appointed government of the Church of England suited monarchs much better. No bishops, no king, was his famous saying. When he became James I of England in 1603, he dashed the hopes of the puritans. There would be no changes in the church. More than that, to ensure the obedience of puritans, the Church of England in 1604 instituted a requirement that all clergymen swear that they believed that every aspect of the church's government and ceremonies was agreeable to the Bible. The strictest nonconforming puritans could not take such an oath. After unsuccessful agitation, up to three hundred puritan clergymen refused to swear and lost their positions.

Marbury does not seem to have been involved in this agitation. Indeed, he appears to have rejected presbyterianism in the early 1590s. That may be why he was allowed to become the minister in Alford in 1594, after having been suspended from his ministry for a number of years. No longer a radical, he started telling his brethren to stop criticizing Elizabeth and her government. A new bishop of London made him minister of a London parish in 1605. In 1607 he was given another London parish, while holding on to the first. Puritans adamantly believed that no minister could properly supervise more than one parish. Pluralists like Marbury were betraying the most sacred duty of a clergyman for the sake of wealth. Marbury died in 1611, leaving behind a comfortable estate.

Anne, in her radical puritanism and her reckless defiance of authority, resembles the young Francis Marbury, not the one who raised her. Among presbyterians, Marbury may have gotten a name as a traitor. They might have applied to him tales they told of other ministers who conformed: how that step of betrayal was only a beginning, how you could see the godliness slowly ebb away from such ministers, even of how they sealed their own damnation by their choice. Perhaps Anne once came across *A Parte of a Register*, where she could contrast the fiery, uncompromising young Francis Marbury with the father who had raised her. Perhaps that encounter helped her decide that no matter what the pressure and possible worldly advantages, nothing could be worse than to compromise God's truth.

———

In 1612, Anne married William Hutchinson, five years older, a puritan and cloth merchant from Alford (historians have argued long and inconclusively about whether specific social groups found puritanism especially attractive). The Hutchinsons had money, but unlike the

Marburys and Drydens, they were not gentry (as was common with the newly affluent, the Hutchinsons tried to prove that their ancestry entitled them to a coat of arms, but the royal herald rejected their claim). William and his brothers were ambitious and educated. One of them grew wealthy enough to bear the loss of a substantial fortune in the great London fire of 1666.

Anne Hutchinson gave birth to the first of fifteen children a little more than nine months after the wedding. She was to give birth every year or two until 1633. There was nothing unusual in that. What was unusual was the result. Over half of all babies at this time died before reaching the age of three, and one in five mothers died of pregnancy-related complications. Hutchinson lost only three of her children in childhood, and all of them seem to have survived past three. Two of the children died in an outbreak of the plague in 1630 that killed perhaps a fifth of Alford's population. Hutchinson must have had a strong constitution to match the force of her personality, and her subsequent reputation as a healer seems well-founded.

Despite her capacities, she worked within a narrow sphere. Married women had few legal privileges. They could not buy or sell property, make contracts, or sue or be sued. If they earned money, it legally belonged to their husbands. When possible, they were expected to focus on the arduous tasks of being wives, mothers, and household managers. The Bible commanded them to submit to their husbands. Puritan preachers reiterated that command, while complaining how frequently wives ignored it.

However, puritan women's place was not simply one of subordination. Ministers also told husbands that their wives were companions whom it was their duty to love, not their slaves, and they told wives that they need not quietly submit to beatings or adultery. It was a Christian wife's duty to admonish her husband for his failings and a husband's duty to accept admonishment. Ministers warned women that they were not to love and obey their husbands more than Christ. If they had to choose, they were to choose Christ, and England's ecclesiastical courts saw sizable numbers of puritan women who put Christ ahead of any earthly authority.

In the Hutchinson family, it is unlikely that Anne ever had to choose between William and Christ. William respected and loved her and perhaps even felt a sense of social inferiority around her. There are no hints in any of the accounts of Anne, some extremely hostile, that her vigorous independent religious life created any domestic friction.

For the first decade or so of Anne's married life, most puritans adjusted to the status quo in the Church of England fairly easily. Those who swore their oaths to the church, remained quiet, and did not agitate for change were generally overlooked by the authorities. Only twenty miles from Alford, the port of Boston, Lincolnshire, was a hotbed of puritanism. Its minister, John Cotton (1585–1652) was a famous scholar and a tireless and much sought after counselor to both English and continental Protestants. He became a committed non-conformist a few years after taking up his Boston post in 1612. Bribes and courteous stalling kept the Bishop of Lincoln from paying too much attention while Cotton and his followers ignored the practices of the Church of England of which they disapproved. William Hutchinson's business would certainly have taken him to Boston on market days, and Anne might have accompanied him to hear the famous Cotton preaching, or she might have gone on her own. Determined puritans would travel many miles along the deeply rutted and at times almost impassable roads of England to hear their favorite preachers, and we know that Anne admired Cotton greatly.

Or she might not have felt the need to travel so far. In 1624, another admirer of Cotton, John Wheelwright (1592–1679), was appointed minister of Anne's neighboring village of Bilsby. Wheelwright was a bellicose man, renowned as a student at Cambridge University for his wrestling skill and fierce football playing. In 1630, he married William Hutchinson's youngest sister, Mary. Anne had ample help in the pursuit of her religious life.

———

One of the central issues of Hutchinson's religious life, indeed, of the religious life of all puritans, was how she could know if she had been saved and would go to heaven. That personal issue constituted one small part of a vast cosmic drama, revealed, puritans believed, by the Bible.

Before time began, God (a trinity, the Father, Son, and Holy Spirit, but at the same time one God) decided to create human beings. Puritans, following the great Protestant John Calvin (1509–64), held that God unalterably willed, or predestined, that most of these still-uncreated

{ *The Times and Trials of Anne Hutchinson* }

humans would go to hell as a demonstration of His justice. A very few, the elect, would go to heaven as a demonstration of his mercy.

To enact this plotline, God created the world. He made an agreement, the covenant of works, with the first man Adam in the Garden of Eden. Under this covenant, as long as Adam (and Eve) continued to perfectly obey God's will, God promised that they and all their posterity would continue in perfect happiness. But tempted by the devil, they ate the fruit that God had forbidden to them. They thereby broke the covenant of works, as God predestined.

Adam and Eve's sinful act destroyed their original holiness. Ever since, everyone has been born with original sin. We are in our nature totally corrupt. No matter what good we might do, our hearts are full of evil and selfishness that can break out at any time. We all deserve to go to hell because of our innate wickedness, and that is where all those people God predestined for damnation end up (damned babies got the easiest room in hell, proclaimed a popular Massachusetts poem). Although the covenant of works is still in effect, no one can fulfill its terms and be perfectly holy, because everyone sins. People who try to be saved to the slightest degree by their own piety or deeds will invariably fail and go to hell.

For the tiny number of us whom God predestined for salvation, he made a covenant of grace. Jesus on the cross took the guilt of their sin and absorbed the punishment it deserves. They are spared hell not because of anything they do but because of Christ's sacrifice. The elect are saved by God's free grace (His eternal favor and goodwill), not by their own works.

When all the predestined elect have been born and saved, Christ will return for the Last Judgment. The world and time will come to an end, while heaven and hell will endure for eternity as monuments to God's glory, mercy, and justice.

———

How does this vast epic intersect with ordinary people? They go about their lives paying little attention to the cosmic drama in which they are embedded. Perhaps they are lukewarm Christians, leading a more or less good life, complacent and convinced that Christ is their savior. But at some point, perhaps through the fiery preaching of a puritan minister, one of these lukewarm Christians might realize that she has not really scrutinized herself and not really faced a deeply buried smugness, a sense that she is fundamentally good. She is still under a covenant of works, still convinced deep down, even unconsciously, that she will go to heaven because she deserves to. That is a sure sign, she realizes, that she is in a covenant of works and is going to hell.

At this point, panic and terror set in. The once complacent Christian starts to discover the extraordinary hollowness of her good behavior and the endless depths of her sinful nature. The more she discovers, the wider and more awful the distance between her and God feels. If the person in whom this is happening is in the covenant of grace and predestined to be saved, then this process is all to the good. Only the gut-wrenching personal discovery of how incapable humans are of saving themselves prepares them to truly depend on Christ for salvation.

The very moment in this agonizing process that genuine, total dependence on Christ occurs is the moment of conversion, and in that twinkling of an eye, a number of complex supernatural events take place. Through God's free grace, the convert receives true faith that Christ died for her. As part of the same event, God justifies her. Justification is an edict that because of Christ's sacrifice, God absolves the convert of the guilt of her sins. Henceforth, she is in His eyes just, and she may go to heaven. God then begins changing her corrupt human nature by making it truly holy, in a process called sanctification. That process is partial; no human can become perfectly holy in this lifetime.

Predestination might seem grossly arbitrary and unfair. Puritans, however, insisted that the comfort it gave the elect was unmeasurable. Once your membership in the covenant of grace had been confirmed by justification, you could have assurance of salvation. If God had predestined you to heaven, then, regardless of whether you sinned again, you would get there. God would not change His mind. Assurance was the safe harbor after the emotional storms of conversion, and, puritans claimed, it brought with it the most profound peace and joy that life gave. Puritans delighted to point out that since their foes the Catholics did not believe in predestination, they could only ever hope they were saved. Scholars have claimed that transformations as sweeping as the rise of capitalism and the beginnings of modern science were jump-started by the incalculably powerful psychological effects of the Calvinist doctrine of assurance of salvation.

But how was an ordinary puritan like Hutchinson supposed to read God's mind? The stakes were dizzyingly high: heaven, if you found assurance; hell, perhaps, if you did not, and you knew that most people went to hell. When Hutchinson was a girl, puritan ministers worked out the solution that remained conventional for the seventeenth century: look at yourself closely and unflinchingly. If you found convincing signs of genuine sanctification and faith — your pious thoughts, for example, your struggles against sin, your good deeds, and your reliance on Christ — you could trust that God had justified and saved you.

Ministers, however, also endlessly stressed that blind, sin-drenched human beings easily fooled themselves that they had real faith in Jesus when they did not and that their holiness was God-given when in fact it came from their own efforts. Such sinners, ministers warned, were unconsciously still in a covenant of works, trying to save themselves by their own efforts, rather than in a covenant of grace, relying completely on Christ and God's free grace for salvation. Moreover, the ministers cautioned that no matter how much you were sure you were saved, if your zeal started to flag or you lapsed into sin, you needed to question that assurance. The ministers' mixed message, giving assurance with one hand and snatching it away with the other, too often left confused puritans lost in mazes of intense doubt and fear.

In response to this dilemma, Hutchinson's Lincolnshire neighbor John Cotton around 1630 came up with a radically different route to assurance of salvation: do not rely on your changing and difficult-to-interpret moods and behavior but on God alone, via the Bible. There are scripture verses that, to puritans, made direct, absolute promises of salvation: Isaiah 43:25, for example, "For mine own sake will I put away thy transgressions," or 1 Timothy 1:15. "Jesus Christ came into the world to save sinners, of which I am chief."

You might have heard and mulled over such a verse many times. But at some point, according to Cotton, if you were among the saved, you would experience it as having a new, compelling power, as if it were speaking to you directly. That power came from its now being in fact a personal message from God carried by the Holy Spirit. Cotton called this message the immediate witness, or seal, of the Spirit.

Words in the verse like "thy transgressions" or "I am chief" now referred to you personally, and God was thereby revealing to you that He had saved you. Because of the darkness of the human mind, you might not notice these revelations at first. But Cotton promised they would continue and eventually bring us to unspeakable joy.

After a Christian had learned by this direct communication that she was saved, she could examine herself for signs of holiness to confirm her salvation, as a kind of reality check. But Cotton insisted that anyone subsequently doubting their salvation had to experience the witness of the Spirit again before they could again trust those signs. A few other ministers spoke of the witness of the Spirit, but for them, it was a rare event and experienced only after people had discovered the signs of their holiness, not before. Thus, if someone chose to make an issue of it, Cotton's way of finding assurance could appear dangerously incompatible with conventional methods, for it might delude people into neglecting holiness in pursuit of a sort of mystical bliss, with grave personal and social consequences. Conversely, from Cotton's perspective, the conventional methods might appear to lead people away from God, not toward him, and thereby damn souls and betray the Reformation. Cotton, however, was widely respected and mild. He was also fairly nonjudgmental, as puritans went, and in that critical way, he differed sharply from Anne Hutchinson.

———

We know a little about Hutchinson's spiritual life in England because she revealed some of its details during her civil trial in Massachusetts in 1637. Just as Cotton taught, she found assurance of salvation when God sent her an absolute promise of salvation, apparently sometime around 1630. Subsequently, she tried to reinforce her assurance by the evidence of her sanctification. This attempt resulted in a spiritual crisis. God showed her the "atheism" of her heart, for she had sought spiritual comfort in her own pious thoughts and good works rather than in Christ. She had turned, she decided, to a covenant of works for assurance. The crisis left Hutchinson with an abiding suspicion of conventional puritan methods of finding assurance.

English culture was still semimagical. Most people, whether they were illiterate or received a university degree, believed in witches and ghosts, portents and prophecies. Some people used the Bible for fortune-telling.

For Hutchinson, the verses that told her of her salvation, Jeremiah 46:27, 28, told her a great deal besides. "I will make a full end of all the nations whither I have driven thee," God prophesied to Hutchinson through them, "but I will not make a full end of thee."

God meant two things with this prophecy, Hutchinson concluded. The first was that He would destroy England for its denial of true religion. Such a message made a great deal of sense around 1630. King James had died in 1625. His son, Charles I, proved an even more authoritarian ruler. He initiated a gradually escalating crackdown on puritanism, and he had little love for Parliament, which responded to his requests, he felt, with insufficient obedience. Charles married a French Catholic princess and coerced money from his subjects. Puritans rapidly began to see a sinister conspiracy at work, in which Catholic agents aimed to exterminate both Protestantism and English liberties. In response, radical puritans in 1627 began planning the Massachusetts Bay Colony as a puritan refuge.

The second thing God meant in the verses from Jeremiah was that Hutchinson enjoyed divine protection; God would not make a full end of her. That promise of divine protection later gave Hutchinson courage to undertake the risky voyage to Massachusetts, and it would finally lead her to her death.

A few years afterward, probably around 1633, Hutchinson connected her own spiritual experiences to a larger insight about the Church of England. By this time, she was so upset about the rapidly increasing antipuritanism of the church that she felt herself "like to have turned separatist." Separatists were puritans who decided that they could not wait any longer for the Church of England to change and separated from it to start churches of their own (the "Pilgrims" who founded Plymouth colony in New England in 1620 were separatists). Separating from the Church of England, even in the fraught circumstances of the 1630s, was frowned upon by most puritans — it was the religious equivalent of renouncing your allegiance to king and country — and Hutchinson fasted for a day for the better "pondering of the thing."

For her fast, Hutchinson probably shut herself up in her bedroom, after giving instructions to her servants and turning the care of the younger children over to her teenage daughter Faith. As she prayed and meditated, God sent her more scripture messages. They confirmed what she probably already suspected: most ministers, except for Cotton and Wheelwright, did not preach with the voice of the risen Christ. Puritan ministers preached with the voice of John the Baptist, who died before Christ. Limited in their knowledge of Christ, like John, most puritan ministers taught their listeners to find assurance of salvation through human activities like faith and sanctification, not through an encounter with the divine, like Cotton.

Some ministers, Hutchinson ominously learned, preached with an even more dangerous voice, that of Antichrist. Antichrist was a diabolical figure who fooled the world into worshiping a false Christ while persecuting true Christians. Puritans, who agreed that the pope was the Antichrist, saw Antichrist's evil influence emanating from the Church of England itself, through its bishops, ceremonies, and inadequate preachers. The Gospel of Matthew warned that Antichrist's power would grow as the end of the world approached, and there was general agreement in Europe that the end was very near. Antichrist would finally appear so similar to Christ that he would be able to deceive the saints themselves (meaning puritans). It was in Massachusetts, probably, that Hutchinson discovered who preached with the voice of Antichrist.

Hutchinson, strong and self-confident to start with, had that self-confidence increased by her revelations. She never again doubted that God had important things to communicate to her, and she told an acquaintance that "she never had any great thing done about her but it was revealed to her before hand." Hutchinson was now a prophet.

But she was a prophet who still wished to hear the voice of Christ. Unfortunately, Cotton received a summons from the dreaded ecclesiastical Court of High Commission in the summer of 1632. Rather than face a possible jail term, he fled Boston, Lincolnshire, although he would not arrive in Massachusetts for another year. His forced departure was taken as a grim omen by puritans, who all across England prayed for him. Hutchinson certainly would have seen in Cotton's flight a sign of the imminent destruction of England by an angry God.

Puritans frequently immigrated to Massachusetts in family and neighborhood groups and ideally with a minister. Something of the sort seems to have been intended around Alford at the end of 1632 after Cotton left Boston, but the plan went awry. Wheelwright tried to sell his ministry in Bilsby back to its patron. That effort, however, instead of producing funds for travel, got him convicted for simony (the sale of church offices). Nonetheless, large numbers of his relatives, friends, and neighbors began arriving in Massachusetts six months later (Wheelwright himself did not reach the colony until 1636). Had Wheelwright arrived with them, he and his followers, including Hutchinson, would have started their own church in an out-of-the-way town site, and we might not know much about any of them.

Anne and William finally left England in the summer of 1634, with the encouragement of another scripture verse sent to Anne. They, along with eight of their children and an unknown number of servants, journeyed to London to book passage on the ship *Griffin*. They were typical among passengers to Massachusetts in that they traveled as a family group. They were also typical in that the group was leaving for religious reasons, even if most members of the group as individuals were leaving because William and Anne decided to go (25 percent of Massachusetts immigrants in the 1630s were servants, and 50 percent were under eighteen). In London they would have purchased a wide range of supplies for the other side of the ocean: barrels of beef, cheese, vinegar, salt, butter, grain, trunks of clothing, tools of all varieties, and all the building materials they would need for their new house in Massachusetts except for wood and bricks. William undoubtedly brought with him fabrics to sell in Massachusetts. The cost of transportation for the group and their supplies might have been around 150 pounds, or perhaps a year's income for William (two years' income for a fortunate clergyman or a prosperous farmer).

Hutchinson did not hide her talents as the *Griffin* beat its way across the Atlantic in the summer of 1634. She prophesied the date the ship would arrive at the Massachusetts port of Boston, for which one of the passengers, the Reverend Zechariah Simmes, rebuked her. Simmes subsequently preached to the passengers that love of one's fellow Christians demonstrated justification, probably a good thing to remind them of on the crowded, hot, stinking ship. Hutchinson, however, heard in his preaching too much John the Baptist—like emphasis on holiness and not enough on Christ. She started explaining to the other passengers Simmes's deficiencies. When Simmes confronted her, Hutchinson warned him that "when she came to Boston there would be something more seen than [Simmes] said." Moreover, according to Simmes, she portentously cited Christ's speech of John

16:12, "I have many things to say but you cannot bear them now." Simmes decided that Hutchinson was a person of narrow and corrupt opinions, a reasonable enough reaction, given the provocation, and one that before long would be widely shared.

Perhaps Hutchinson had entertained hopes about Massachusetts as a promised land for God's chosen people such as herself. But what she saw as her boat pulled into Boston harbor did not look like Zion. On a small peninsula, marshland and pastures filled with tree stumps surrounded three small hills, on which sprawled a raw, four-year-old town with around eight hundred inhabitants. Some people still lived in thatched-roofed, wood-lined holes in the ground. The simplest houses were one-room shacks covered with clay and animal manure, possessing thatched roofs and wooden chimneys. Governor Winthrop, however, had a four-room, two-story house, while the richest man in the colony, Hutchinson's future ally William Coddington, had built his family a house of brick. Other prosperous and industrious settlers were starting to lower the chances of their dwellings burning down by shingling their roofs and replacing wooden chimneys with stone ones.

For a woman coming from a life of prosperity, Massachusetts was a shock. Hutchinson told one of her fellow travelers that if God had not revealed to her that England would be destroyed, her heart would have sunk at the sight of Boston. It was a prophetic warning to which she should have paid more attention.

CHAPTER 2

Disciplinarians
Massachusetts, 1630–1636

What Hutchinson could not have known as she gazed out at the drab, ramshackle town was that behind the grim material scene lay the realization of what radical puritans considered an ideal society. Not a utopia, for puritans had too deep a sense of human sin to imagine perfect societies. But what they had created by the time she arrived was the fulfillment of their goal for England — a "godly" commonwealth, in which church and state served as vehicles for the institution of one of the most emphasized terms in the puritan vocabulary: "discipline." Hutchinson would quickly make herself an important, although problematic, participant in the Massachusetts disciplinary project.

In the sixteenth century, "discipline" was the rallying cry of radical puritans like the presbyterians, so much so that their opponents called them "disciplinarians." To understand what Massachusetts was about, we need to understand what the term meant to them. Discipline, in a narrow sense, was the formal and informal guidance and correction that church officers and ordinary members offered each other in order to protect the holiness and purity of their churches and keep each other on the path to heaven.

In a broad sense, discipline was the maintenance of the moral and spiritual fiber of society, and not only the churches but virtually every institution within society, from the government to the courts to the schools to the family, participated in it. Discipline required punishment (often in large doses) to maintain order, teach the evil of sin and heresy, and avoid God's wrath, in the form of plagues, famines, invasions, and other disasters. But its goal was to knit together a Christian community in what puritans understood to be harmony and love. One of a puritan minister's proudest claims was that his parishioners seldom sued each other.

Presbyterians argued that discipline was critical for a flourishing country. A disciplined population was a moral, peaceful, and well-ordered one, pleasing to God and advantageous to a nation's prosperity. Complained one Elizabethan of presbyterian sales tactics, "If discipline were planted [the presbyterians claimed], there would be no vagabonds, no beggars, a thing very plausible; and in like manner they promised the people many of the impossible wonders of their discipline." Presbyterians pointed to the decline of Athens and Rome, due, it was commonly believed, to lack of discipline, to argue how important their "discipline" was to England.

When possible in England, puritans attempted to implement social discipline as best they could. Followers of the minister John White, for example, an active promoter of immigration to New England, took control of the Dorchester town government in the 1610s. Drinking, dancing, and illegitimate births declined, educational opportunities expanded, church attendance was enforced, and the town set up an extremely progressive welfare system.

The legal systems of both church and state were major vehicles for discipline. In England, both systems were, in the eyes of puritans, hopelessly inadequate. The Church of England disciplined sin erratically at best, through a complex and frequently corrupt set of courts and legal procedures, many of which went back to Roman Catholicism. Money too often served as the lubricant of the system and as a substitute for repentance. Church courts were tangled in matters that puritans regarded as secular, like marriage and wills. Some of them had the power to hand out what puritans regarded as secular, not spiritual punishments, like fines and imprisonments, and they imposed these all too frequently on nonconforming puritans. The secular courts themselves were a no less complex tangle of overlapping jurisdictions. They were cumbersome and, like the church courts, too easily greased with money. The founders of Massachusetts, by contrast, intended their colony to have an interlocked system of discipline in the churches and the state as close to ideal as they could make it.

Puritans called church discipline the wall that protected churches from the corruption of the world. The immigrants quickly built that wall higher than presbyterians back in England had advocated. It was hard to join a Massachusetts church. A church began when a group of men who had approved each other for their holiness swore a covenant committing themselves to be faithful members of a biblically sound church. They would then elect the pastor, in charge of discipline, the teacher, in charge of doctrine (but some churches had only one minister), and the ruling lay elders. All subsequent members had to take the covenant. But first the congregation examined them to learn if they were good Christians. These exams grew progressively stricter, and by the mid-1630s, applicants had to testify to the congregation about the processes within them that demonstrated that God had justified them. Show that you were probably saved, and the congregation accepted you as a "visible saint" (a saint was someone who was certainly going to heaven). The churches recognized themselves as parts of the Church of England (to which all English people automatically belonged), but no puritans arriving from England could take communion with them or have their children baptized until they had joined a Massachusetts church. This exclusivity enraged their puritan brethren back home.

Once in a Massachusetts church, all members, male and female, were expected to take responsibility for discipline. They were to keep a lively interest in each other, share their spiritual experiences, give advice, and when necessary criticize each other for moral and spiritual lapses. It was within that larger disciplinary process that Massachusetts church legal proceedings took place. If members saw a fellow member erring, they would speak to them in private. If that failed to produce results, they went to the church's elders. The elders investigated, and if they could not resolve the problem, they prepared a disciplinary proceeding for the whole congregation. The elders rarely brought a proceeding this far along unless there was likely to be a consensus in the congregation that the member in question had sinned. The hearing was to determine the nature of the sin, the extent to which the member felt repentant for the sin, and what the appropriate consequence should be. The accused would fend questions from the members of the congregation (women were ordinarily expected to put their questions through men) and from the elders. The male members of the congregation voted at the end, and most congregations tried to have unanimous decisions. The goal of the hearing was reintegrating the member successfully back into the church community. Depending on the repentance he or she showed, the consequence might be a grave admonition delivered by one of the ministers, or, if necessary, it might be excommunication, hopefully only for a short while. Sinners might also be given more time to reflect on their sins before the congregation made a final decision.

Secular discipline was the responsibility of secular government. The government of Massachusetts grew out of the charter that King Charles I granted the Massachusetts Bay Company in 1629. This document, like other colonial charters, gave the company the usual organization of a joint-stock business company, with a governor, a deputy governor, a court of assistants (board of directors), and freemen (shareholders). Governor, assistants, and freemen were expected to meet four times a year in the General Court, where the freemen would elect the governor and assistants for the following year and pass such laws and orders as the company needed. The charter also authorized the company to set up a local government in its colony. The only restraint on that government was that it could not act contrary to the laws of England.

One serious problem the Massachusetts Bay Company faced in creating a refuge for puritans was getting a proper leadership across the Atlantic. Puritans had been trying to settle New England for most of the 1620s, and the Massachusetts Bay Company's precursor bequeathed the company the struggling small settlement of Salem. But so far, the region had proved a sinkhole for money, while colonies in their early years were notorious for their high mortality. Thus John Winthrop (1588–1649), an obscure Suffolk gentleman and lawyer, and some other shareholders in the company had a strong hand in 1629 when they approached the company's officers with a proposition. They were willing to risk their lives and fortunes by crossing the Atlantic, but only if their fellow freemen elected them to be the company's new Court of Assistants and they could take the charter with them. With the Court of Assistants and charter of the company in Massachusetts, the colony would be in practice self-governing.

The General Court agreed to the proposition and elected Winthrop governor. At the time, Winthrop's law career was stalled and his financial prospects growing worse. His leadership skills were considerable, however, although still untested (he had been defeated when he ran for parliament in 1624), and he had an unbending devotion to the cause of the colony. Winthrop and the new assistants organized a substantial migration. Eleven ships and around seven hundred settlers went to Massachusetts in 1630. Besides the Court of Assistants, at most only one or two freemen of the company were among the immigrants. Thus, there was no body of freemen in the colony to vote the assistants in and out of office. The Court of Assistants did not seek rule without consent, however, and in October 1630 it made most of the males in the colony freemen. The Court of Assistants originally restricted the new freemen's role to electing the assistants, governor, and deputy governor each year. Even so, unlike in England and the southern colonies, freemen chose the entire membership of the government that directly affected their lives, just as they elected their ministers.

The Court of Assistants, whose members were called magistrates, also served as the initial judicial court in the colony. Besides Winthrop, only a few of the magistrates had legal backgrounds. What they lacked in legal expertise, however, they made up for by their disciplinary zeal. Far more than in colonies like Virginia and Maryland, magistrates spoke of sin and wickedness rather than felonies and misdemeanors. Victims often had to bring crimes to the attention of the southern courts; in Massachusetts, constables and grand juries were eager to report sin to the proper authorities. As with church trials, the magistrates were often at least as interested in acknowledgment of sin as they were in punishment. For noncapital offenses, magistrates often remitted fines upon signs of proper repentance, and, like the ministers, they sometimes let off wrongdoers with a stern admonition. Sometimes they ordered miscreants to make public confession of their sins or to confer with a minister.

In 1634, the freemen demanded to see the charter and then successfully insisted on the legislative rights it gave them. They deputized freemen from each town to join the Court of Assistants to meet in a combined General Court four times a year. The Court of Assistants functioned as an executive body in between sessions of the General Court.

That same year, 1634, the General Court became the colony's primary judicial court. Even after it set up inferior courts in 1636, it often served as the court of first resort. The court decreed in 1634 that in cases involving the death penalty or banishment, it could decide guilt or innocence as well as a jury (although juries were also now used). In the General Court, the same people served as prosecutors, judges, and jury, and cases there could be decided by majority vote. With such forces arrayed against defendants, conviction rates ran extraordinarily high, around 90 percent.

English presbyterians would have been delighted with these disciplinary structures. But the leaders of Massachusetts drove the protection of discipline far past anything an English presbyterian would have dared contemplate. In 1631, the General Court ordered that no one who was not a church member could become a freeman and vote or serve in office. The puritans of Massachusetts now did not just discipline each other in their churches; the male "saints" disciplined their rulers when they voted them in and out of office, and the magistrates disciplined everyone else, along with any saints-turned-criminal, and protected the churches from the corruptions of the world. Massachusetts had created what amounted to a semiautonomous republic of saints in a world governed by monarchs.

The magistrates were swift to punish conventional crimes like murder and theft, as well as individuals such as runaway or disrespectful servants. But by the time Anne Hutchinson arrived, the General Court had also made significant steps in instituting what historians have called a "culture of discipline." They had banned the consumption of tobacco, instituted the death penalty for adultery (with the same penalty for males as females, a radical innovation), and protected the holiness of Sunday (the Sabbath) by giving exceptionally large fines for Sunday drunkenness and by whipping people for shooting birds on that day. The General Court had instructed town constables to report all idle people to it, and it had forbidden what it considered unnecessarily fashionable clothing as a waste of money and as "pernicious to the commonwealth." Opponents of the new order had been banished, one of them after having his ears cut off for his criticisms of church and state. These kinds of measures were not unheard of elsewhere, but in Massachusetts they were distinguished by their extent and the seriousness with which they were enforced.

Unfortunately, this godly commonwealth was born in original sin. The 1629 charter was the successor to a land patent that puritan entrepreneurs had procured in 1628 from the Council for New England. The patent included generous boundaries, perhaps through the conniving of the sympathetic puritan council member the Earl of Warwick. The problem with these boundaries was that they took in territory already granted to the son of Sir Ferdinando Gorges, prime mover behind the Council. Having gone behind Gorges's back to get their patent from the Council, the puritans sealed their dubious acquisition with the royal charter of 1629. An incensed Gorges thereafter devoted much of his energy to having the charter revoked. William Laud, archbishop of Canterbury from 1633, worked tirelessly to see puritanism suppressed throughout Charles's realms, and he threw his support behind Gorges's efforts.

The opening salvo in the attack on Massachusetts's charter reached the colony in June 1634. It took the form of an order from Charles I's Privy Council to return the charter. The General Court ignored the request and instead improved the colony's defenses. That fall, Hutchinson's ship brought a letter announcing the formation of the Royal Commission for Regulating Plantations, headed by Archbishop Laud. The commission had, in principle, final power over all colonies. Rumors spread that a ship with troops was being fitted out to come over and compel the colony to take a governor-general and conform to the Church of England. The General Court set up a war council, drilled the militia, and fortified Boston harbor. To ensure solidarity, it required that all men over the age of twenty take an oath of allegiance to the government. In the summer of 1635, Charles announced his intention to appoint Gorges governor-general, and the attorney general initiated quo warranto court proceedings against the Massachusetts charter with the intention of revoking it.

The external attack might have been expected, but an attack on the godly commonwealth from within certainly was not. Roger Williams was a charismatic young minister whose zealotry sublimely transcended any grounding in practical politics. He had arrived in 1631 and tried to convert the colony to severe separatism. Members of Massachusetts churches, he demanded, were not so much as to set foot in an English church on return visits, and the congregations were to repent that they had ever been associated with the Church of England. Most people in the colony did not desire such an extreme separation, and it would have been a disastrous move for the vital relationship of the colony with puritans in England. Moreover, Williams wanted to drastically restrict the disciplinary powers of the magistrates. He insisted that they had control only over secular matters, not religious ones. The magistrates could not, for example, punish violations of the Sabbath. To tie the hands of the magistrates in this way would have made impossible the disciplinary regime envisioned by the leaders of the colony.

Williams had been tucked safely away in separatist Plymouth colony for a few years, but he returned to Salem at the end of 1633. He added to his old doctrines the argument that the king's grant of land to the colony was void; Massachusetts belonged to the Indians, not the king. At the same time, he argued for the spiritual unlawfulness of the Court's oath of allegiance, and under his influence, a number of colonists refused to take it.

It might seem straightforward for the General Court to prosecute Williams. The charter gave the Court the right to banish people simply because they were an "annoyance," and at the very least, Williams fit that description. Moreover, the concept of free speech was in its infancy, and no English governing body recognized an inherent right of citizens to criticize its actions.

Massachusetts puritan legality, however, did not function so straightforwardly. Massachusetts's leaders wished to create a unified Christian society. Yet at the same time, following the teachings of the great Protestant John Calvin, they believed in a strict separation of church and state. For disciplinary purposes, church and state were conceived of roughly as two equally important police bureaus with authority in spheres that were kept separate. Unlike in England, ministers, while they had great influence, could not serve in public offices, and the churches could not give secular punishments such as fines and imprisonment. In England, the state constantly meddled with the Church of England. The monarch was its head, appointed its bishops, and had to approve any changes to its practices or doctrine. Puritans themselves periodically tried to reform the Church of England through parliamentary statutes. The Massachusetts government was supposed to protect the churches, but although run by "saints," it was not supposed to interfere with their religious life.

Williams was a puritan and a church member, and his arguments about oaths, the power of the magistrates, and the charter were all ultimately religious ones. This meant that his offenses, if any, were in the first instance spiritual offenses. Spiritual offenses were the business of the churches, and it was the responsibility of Williams's church to deal with him. Doing so would have required the elders of the church trying to persuade Williams of his errors and bringing him to a formal church trial if he refused to give them up.

Unfortunately, in Salem, Williams was extremely popular. Not only was the church unprepared to convince him of his errors; in the summer of 1634, it unofficially made him its teacher. Had the Massachusetts puritans adopted the conventional English presbyterian model for their churches, Salem's bullheadedness would still not have presented a serious problem. A meeting of the churches would have had the power to summon Williams, debate his ideas with him, formally disown them, and order the Salem church to discipline him.

The Massachusetts puritans, however, believed that no church or body of churches had authoritative power over any other church. A synod (meeting) of churches could advise a church, but it could not order it to do anything. In this respect, their system had mutated so much from standard English presbyterianism that it would shortly acquire a new name, congregationalism. The idea of congregationalism came from the separatists. In the early seventeenth century, some puritans tentatively endorsed congregational theory, probably because the independence it gave each church seemed like an iron-clad defense against the oppression of the bishops. In the initial days of the colony, the Massachusetts puritans almost certainly did not imagine that they might have to face a runaway church.

Williams and Salem proved that this assumption was dangerously wrong. In response, Massachusetts's ministers and magistrates began to tighten up the relationship between the churches and state. On March 4, 1635, the General Court asked the elders of the churches to consider how far the magistrates could intervene in church affairs in the interest of order and peace. Led by Cotton, the teacher at the Boston church since late 1633, the ministers declared that magistrates could defend the true worship of God. The Salem church defiantly replied that even if a church adopted the most grievous heresies, including familism (see below), and refused to reform itself after being convinced of its error by other churches, the magistrates still could not touch it. Rubbing its point in, it officially ordained Williams as its teacher. Cotton requested that the General Court hold off any response while he and his two ruling lay elders sent Salem an admonition confuting its assertion.

The admonition produced no change of heart, and the General Court called Williams before it in July, with the ministers present. The ministers affirmed that Williams's opinions were dangerously erroneous and that the magistrates could intervene. But how, exactly, without crossing the church/state divide? What the Court did was to create a secular legal issue out of the behavior of the Salem church. Salem appointed Williams when it knew that the Court was unhappy with him. That action, the Court argued, constituted contempt for the Court, and the Court withheld a grant of land from Salem as punishment. Salem understandably saw the Court's maneuver as a violation of the divinely mandated separation of church and state. It responded by sending letters to the other churches accusing the magistrates and deputies of a heinous sin for intruding in the churches' sphere, and a sin that invited God's vengeance.

For the General Court, the Salem letter constituted yet further contempt for its authority. In September, it suspended Salem's deputies until the majority of the freemen of the town (the church members, in other words) disclaimed the church's letter. The assistant from Salem, John Endicott, hastily reconsidered his own defiant defense of the letter when threatened with jail. Williams severely damaged his support at Salem by issuing an ultimatum to the church that it separate from the other churches or he would leave it. In October, the Court summoned Williams again. The ministers spent a great deal of time fruitlessly trying to convince him again that he was wrong. After they failed, the Court sentenced him to banishment on the ground that his opinions endangered its authority. Cotton apparently took the lead among the ministers in arguing for Williams's banishment. The Salem church then voted to excommunicate him, thereby giving spiritual approval to the Court's secular decision.

The protracted judicial and ecclesiastical campaign against Williams was in many ways a dry run for the campaign that brought Hutchinson and her allies to trial. It demonstrated that the Massachusetts establishment would protect its unwieldy church-state creation, yet it also showed that such protection would not come easily. Williams's views were clearly incompatible with the goals of the leaders of the colony and perhaps even with the colony's survival. Nonetheless, the campaign against him and his church engendered a steady stream of unease and even resistance. When Salem wrote its letter to the other churches protesting the General Court's actions as a violation of church and state, the Boston elders violated standard procedures. They pocketed the letter rather than read it to the church and have the church discuss what the response should be. Williams claimed that several deputies came to him with tears in their eyes, protesting that they never would have voted to banish him had not Cotton been so insistent. One minister even opposed his banishment. The Court planned to send Williams back to England, but some insider (Williams later claimed it was Winthrop) blanched at the prospect of sending a puritan back to a country increasingly hostile to puritanism. The insider tipped Williams off, and he went to Narragansett Bay, the future Rhode Island, instead.

This hesitation to treat Williams simply as a danger to the colony came from two fundamental elements in the colony's ideological underpinnings. The first was a sense that the state skated on very thin ice in interfering with a church, however much practical sense that interference made. The second was a sense that if puritans stumbled into error on any given issue, they were still part of the community, not enemies, and not quickly to be treated as such. That last sense can be seen not only in the way the Court's actions generated unease but even in the way it and the ministers treated Williams. Both ministers and magistrates worked closely trying to figure out appropriate punitive strategies, but also up to the very last minute they spent a great deal of effort trying to get Williams to change his mind. These were hardheaded men doing what was necessary to keep their colony afloat, but they were also Christians who had the responsibility to reclaim a brother saint, just as in church disciplinary proceedings, not simply punish him. This sense of Williams being part of the spiritual community, however, worked in two directions. He badly undercut his support in Salem when he tried to make the church choose between him and every other church in Massachusetts.

––––––

While Williams threatened the viability of Massachusetts's godly commonwealth, an immigrant who arrived on October 6, 1635, appeared to give it a much-needed bolstering. Henry Vane Jr., born in 1613, was the son of one of the most powerful men in England, a privy councillor to Charles I. An intense conversion experience in his midteens left him assured of his salvation and a puritan. Vane came to New England with Archbishop Laud's blessings; Laud thought it the best place to get puritanism out of his system. With his long hair, aristocratic bearing, and Court associations, Vane fell under suspicion on the boat as a spy sent to betray Massachusetts. Suspicions disappeared, at least for the time being, because he was serious about his puritanism.

Although only twenty-two, Vane deeply impressed the colonists. He was by far the best-connected person to come to Massachusetts — a "noble gentleman," as an initially starstruck Winthrop described him in his journal. England was intensely status conscious, and none of the rulers of Massachusetts came from a rank in society high enough to automatically draw much respect. As one early critic of the government sneered, "The best of them [Winthrop] was but an attorney." Vane's personality reinforced the appeal of his high social status: "a man . . . of a quick conception, and very ready, sharp, and weighty expression . . . which . . . made men think there was somewhat in him extraordinary," as an English enemy later described him.

Vane took up residence in Boston. He liked Cotton enough to build an addition to Cotton's house for himself — it is safe to assume that when the fifty-one-year-old Cotton and his thirty-five-year-old second wife, Sarah, had their prayer sessions, scripture exposition, and meals (with or without their two infants), young Vane was a regular. Almost inevitably, Vane quickly took on a leadership role both in Boston and in the colony. The freemen elected him governor in May 1636, with Winthrop as deputy governor. They must have found Vane attractive at least in part as someone who might be able to provide some protection for the charter. Vane also quickly showed his commitment to preserving a godly commonwealth by writing a letter to the Salem constable warning him to suppress separatist meetings in Salem or face government intervention.

As the Massachusetts disciplinary apparatus grew increasingly fine-honed, Anne Hutchinson made herself a valuable participant in the creation of a godly commonwealth, after a bumpy beginning. Her boatmate, minister Simmes, upon landing in October 1634, went straight to then-governor Thomas Dudley with his concern about Hutchinson. Dudley informed Cotton and Boston's pastor, John Wilson. Cotton and Wilson subjected Hutchinson to a searching interrogation when she applied to join the Boston congregation. Everyone agreed her answers were satisfactory, and the ministers told her that the church did not insist on any one method for assurance of salvation.

Despite Anne's initial difficulty with the church, the Hutchinsons quickly settled into their new community. They built one of the largest houses in Boston across the lane from where Winthrop and his wife, Margaret, lived. Today the famous eighteenth-century Old Corner Bookstore stands on the site of the Hutchinsons' house, a relic of the colonial era surrounded by skyscrapers. William Hutchinson, a successful merchant and thus a "gentleman," by Boston standards, soon became a deputy to the General Court. Thereafter, he took up a number of local offices. Anne, as a gentlewoman, cut an impressive figure with her piety, charity, and neighborliness. Winthrop later said that "her ordinary talke was about the things of the Kingdome of God," and "her usuall conversation was in the way of righteousness and kindnesse." She took a prominent role in helping at births. These were the preeminent exclusively female social occasions and were grave, protracted, and heavily attended events. Childbirth killed up to 20 percent of mothers, and all mothers in labor could expect, in the words of Governor Dudley's poet daughter Anne Bradstreet, "pangs which can't be told by tongue."

As a woman, Hutchinson had little to do directly with formal church disciplinary proceedings, but in the larger sense of church discipline as spiritual counseling and guidance, she quickly carved an important niche for herself. During the long periods of inactivity at births, Hutchinson led the women into discussions about the states of their souls. At this life-or-death time, she explained to them at least as effectively as any minister how easily they could fool themselves that they were in the covenant of grace while they were still in the covenant of works. They might pray frequently and fervently, honor their ministers, and lead morally upright lives. Their activities might even give them moments of great spiritual comfort. And yet, Hutchinson terrifyingly and convincingly warned them, they had never been truly converted. They were unconsciously still relying on their own works to save them, not Christ; she spread a "false terror," Winthrop later sniffed, when he had soured on Hutchinson.

False or not, Hutchinson's fearmongering was effective. John Cotton acknowledged that women, and through them their husbands, "were convinced, that they had gone on in a Covenant of Works, and were much shaken and humbled thereby, and brought to enquire more seriously after the Lord Jesus Christ." Men, as well as women, came to Hutchinson for counsel. Powerfully self-confidant, Hutchinson claimed that if she had a half hour's talk with a man, she would be able to tell if he were among the saved or not. Hutchinson had no reluctance to offer her own advanced spiritual state as a model to these now-serious inquirers. The result, according to Cotton, was initially entirely positive. Hutchinson "wrought with God, and with the Ministers, the work of the Lord. . . [and] found loving and dear respect from both our Church-Elders and Brethren, and so from my self."

Hutchinson's semipublic religious activism and its easy acceptance by both sexes might seem surprising, the more so since some writers on Hutchinson portray her as functioning within an environment that was totally oppressive to women who asserted their gifts. Yet Hutchinson was no aberration. English society took for granted that women were a weaker sex, more emotional and less capable of reason than men, although perhaps more religious, and it laid out very narrow roles for them. Nonetheless, social godliness such as Anne Hutchinson's was a career for puritans that, if not gender neutral, was open to the talented of both sexes. A visibly pious woman, not averse to displaying her advanced spiritual status and capacities, curious about other people, willing and eager to offer them counsel, and admired for her general good judgment could accrue a great deal of respect, among ministers as well as the laity.

Carving out an ostensibly private but de facto semipublic role for herself, Hutchinson was following a well-beaten path. It was certainly helpful if a woman as visible as she was kept herself relatively protected from criticism about neglecting her wifely calling, and Hutchinson had an admiring and supportive husband and enough servants to keep the family's domestic affairs above reproach. Had Hutchinson been her father's son instead of his daughter, she almost certainly would have gone on to a career as a minister, but part of the attraction of puritanism to women, and to lay men, for that matter, was that it did provide considerable room for what amounted to a vocational lay ministry.

Hutchinson's impressive service to discipline in this godly commonwealth took place in the colony's most important church. Boston's central location on the coast and its ideal deepwater harbor ensured that it became the main town for commerce and communication with the rest of the world. The church routinely shared its meetinghouse with the General Court (puritans did not think that buildings could be sacred), and people from all over the colony came to Boston to attend the Court's sessions and to sell produce and buy goods. Immigrants disembarked in Boston, and they usually lodged in Boston households when they first arrived. Boston's church was "the most publick, where Seamen and all Strangers came."

Boston's church not only was the most public in the colony but also might have been the most successful. Membership in the church grew by more than 50 percent in the first four months of Cotton's stay, from roughly 80 to more than 120 men and women, in a town of perhaps 500 people. Winthrop, a proud member of the church, exulted that "more were converted & added to that Churche, than to all the other Churches in the Baye." As the Williams episode demonstrated, the elders of the Boston church provided leadership to the entire colony. The eminent piety of Boston's lay members from this period was remembered down to the end of the century, as was the strictness of its discipline under pastor John Wilson and ruling lay elder Leverett. The Boston church, in its highly visible sanctity and exemplary moral supervision, approached the puritan ideal of a Christian community. The Massachusetts historian William Hubbard, a young teenager at the time, claimed that some people believed the Boston church to be "in so flourishing a condition as were scarce any where else to be paralleled."

To its members, the Boston church, with its spiritual vibrancy and strict discipline, embodied the purpose of coming to Massachusetts. Some were so enthusiastic that they began to entertain extraordinary hopes for their congregation in the mid-1630s. Mainstream Christianity conceived of history as sliding downhill from bad to worse, until Jesus returned in his Second Coming and ended it altogether. From the beginning of the seventeenth century, an alternative conception of the end of time, millenarianism, had been circulating among puritans. This was a positive vision of the Last Days in which

Antichrist would be overthrown, the Jews would all be converted to Christianity, and then in the aura of Christ's approach, a "glorious church" would arise and last for up to a thousand years. The great puritan scholar Perry Miller argued that the original migration to Massachusetts was itself a millenarian errand in the wilderness to create a model church for the end of time. That argument has been rejected by scholars, but as the New Englanders' early church arrangements grew more confident, they could begin to interpret their project as part of the approach of the millennium. At least some Bostonians saw their church in this way and, indeed, deemed it, according to William Hubbard, in a phrase loaded with millenarian overtones, "the most glorious church in the world."

———

It was around a half year after Vane arrived that we have the first indication that strange theological opinions were circulating in this glorious church. Some sources indicate that Vane, who later demonstrated that he had a prodigious appetite for radical theology, introduced these opinions. Some suggest that Hutchinson introduced at least some of them. Others suggest that a number of people brought them over. We do know that Hutchinson applied her considerable intellectual powers and persuasive gifts to them, and that Vane successfully encouraged her to set up meetings at her house, one of the biggest in Boston, to discuss theology.

Hutchinson's circle enthusiastically endorsed Cotton's conception of assurance through revelations. Orthodox puritans, including Cotton, however, argued that conversion brought about a divinely induced transformation of the human nature of the believer, measured by faith and sanctification. Hutchinson and her circle speculated, by contrast, that conversion was an annihilation of the earthly by the divine. Christ did not transform believers; He took them over. Instead of being guided by their own will, believers were continually guided by the Holy Spirit, and, ideally, they would experience ceaseless joy.

Such speculation might seem harmless today, but it came with a loaded history. Most of these concepts can be traced back to rogue puritan ministers in England. They preached the bliss of assurance of salvation that came with union with the divine, and they rejected the emphasis within mainstream puritan divinity on the linkage of assurance with uncertainty, sustained zeal, and long and painful introspection. They got into mutually vituperative quarrels with mainstream puritan ministers, whom they accused of making assurance so difficult in order to magnify their own importance. Identifying themselves as the true torchbearers of the Reformation, the real "puritans," in other words, these preachers would gain access to a pulpit for a while or preach in houses. Their followers were frequently poached from more conventional puritan ministers.

They often found themselves on the run, hounded by the bishops and puritans alike. They were hounded with this intensity in part because they had grafted on to the Calvinist theological framework of the Church of England ideas with a particularly tainted ancestry. These went back to the murderous, polygamous, revelation-driven radical Protestant Anabaptists who assumed mad, bloody control of Münster, Germany, in 1535 (the Anabaptists were then bloodily massacred by Catholic troops). The Anabaptists' Spirit-inspired revelations had in turn inspired a heretical group puritans especially loathed, the Family of Love. Familists believed that Christians under the illumination of the Holy Spirit could eventually enjoy revelations, perfect union with God, and freedom from both sin and the responsibility for it.

In England, the Family of Love flourished illegally as a small sect in the Elizabethan and early Jacobean period, and puritan ministers were its earliest and most vocal opponents. Familism encompassed a host of heresies, most immediately antinomianism (freedom from having to obey God's laws), which itself was enough to conjure up images of moral anarchy. Even worse, and more critically, members of this sect blasphemously believed that their own revelations superseded the Bible altogether. For conventional Protestants, the Bible formed the sole foundation of the church and of salvation. Any revelation claiming to supersede it could come only from the devil or from a sinful imagination, and it could only result in evil conduct and the rejection of the lawful authority of ministers and rulers. Real English Familists seem to have been a quiet, decorous group, but in the English imagination, anything associated with familism was inseparable from Münster, massacres, immorality, and blasphemy. It is no accident that the Salem church cited familism when stressing how low a church could sink without the magistrates being able to interfere.

There is no evidence that suggests that committed radicals in the Boston congregation were a large group. One can see why they, as puritans, would have been proud of their church, with its strict discipline and famous teacher. Puritanism, however, is not usually associated with broad-mindedness. Why would the Boston church tolerate ideas suggestive of antinomianism and, even worse, familism?

Devout Boston puritans could esteem and love radicals like Vane and Hutchinson because there was much in them to admire. Vane helped to suppress Salem separatism. One of Hutchinson's most hostile critics, the minister Thomas Weld, admitted that the radicals "would appeare very humble, holy, and spirituall Christians . . . they would deny themselves farre, speake excellently, pray with such soule-ravishing expression." You could learn from their strict, heartfelt piety without worrying that they were planning a bloodbath. Conversely, it would take a great deal of provocation to imagine bringing one of them before a disciplinary hearing. Vane helped to suppress Salem separatism.

Another reason to give someone pause before bringing a radical before a disciplinary hearing was the social status of the leading radicals. Vane was not someone to alienate. (He became even more important when he returned to England, which is why official histories of the controversy avoided discussing him. The reliance of scholars on those histories explains why his role is downplayed in modern accounts of Hutchinson; Vane's contemporaries, when they were feeling less exposed, were angrily blunt about his importance.) The Hutchinsons, in both nuclear and extended form, were one of the leading families in Boston.

Moreover, radicals went to some trouble to fit in. They claimed not to differ from Cotton in their beliefs, and where they did go astray, they trod delicately. Hutchinson, for example, up to her civil trial in November 1637, presented her own opinions as questions, not assertions, at least to anyone whom she was not certain agreed with her. Cotton said that when radicals offered him unorthodox scripture interpretations, they claimed to be unsettled about them. A Bostonian recalled much later that "the Serpents subtilty shew'd it self in a Multitudinarism of Questions, started under pretence of seeking light." While the radicals' claim to unsettledness was undoubtedly deceptive, it was self-deceptive, at least in part, a way for them to blend into the larger puritan community that they valued. Weld noted that when radicals found themselves disagreeing with others, they would say, "I doe meane even as you doe, you and I are both of one minde in substance, and differ onely in words." Conventionally, a heretic was someone who stoutly asserted damnable opinions, not a pious, neighborly, disciplined church member who asked questions about the meaning of scripture.

Boston would be an especially easy congregation for such radicals to belong to because of Cotton himself. It was an extraordinary twist of misfortune that the most important, most visible church in the colony managed to have probably the most unconventional of all prominent puritan ministers. The radicals did not stick out obviously in Boston because Cotton's teaching about assurance through progressively more intense revelations of the Holy Spirit was already so unusual. Hutchinson only needed to bend his ideas slightly and surround them with a fog of questions to insinuate her own position. As was discussed earlier, there was a difference, and a difference that could be magnified as critical. But one had to look quite hard to find it and had to have pressing reasons to do so, which probably simply was not the case for many people.

The coherence of the Boston congregation thus came from unusually lenient standards of orthodoxy, mutual forbearance, common standards of behavioral expectations, a well-functioning, satisfying church, and a shared sense at least among some of the congregation of the impending Kingdom of God and Boston's role therein. These factors were powerful enough to make differences in theology petty and provisional. If a few radicals went a bit off the deep end temporarily in their discovery of God's free grace, it was for a good cause. Cotton for a long time assumed that they were basically sound and would eventually settle into his version of orthodoxy. In the meantime, he dismissed their peculiar terminology as "misexpressions." The radicals, in turn, as Cotton later remarked, hoped that the rest of their godly brothers and sisters would catch up with them.

The success of the Boston church points to a sometimes overlooked element in puritanism. Tolerance for linguistic idiosyncrasies among people perceived as godly could override commitments to doctrinal uniformity. As will be seen, reports of doctrinal deviance began coming out of Boston very early in 1636. But Boston's pastor John Wilson, later to be reviled by most of the congregation, went a long time before he decided that the errors were serious enough to require a response. After the affair had died down, he showed himself more tolerant of Boston's theological peculiarities than some of his ministerial brethren, and the same was true of his soon-to-be embattled partner in the Boston church, John Winthrop. Purging people you disagreed with was one way to maintain community; another, as Winthrop once advised, was to learn from them where possible and "cover the rest with love." We know from the records of one of the few puritan churches of this time, in the English community in Amsterdam, that the elders of the church practiced remarkable patience with members expressing ideas that had long been regarded as heretical. The Boston church could approve the radicals' considerable virtues, agree with their admiration for Cotton, hope that they would grow out of their misexpressions, and stay focused on the coming millennium. But what to one puritan were "misexpressions" might be to another damnable and dangerous heresies. It would soon become clear that others less charitable among the increasingly vigilant disciplinarians of Massachusetts had a much darker understanding of what was going on in Boston.

CHAPTER 3

Secret Quarrels

Spring–Fall 1636

Shortly before Vane sailed to Massachusetts in the summer of 1635, another immigrant boat departed. Passengers included the thirty-year-old minister Thomas Shepard, his wife, and his baby son, along with some of his followers. This was Shepard's second attempt to cross the Atlantic and leave behind him a turbulent English career. He flirted with Familism while an undergraduate at Cambridge University. His first job, as a temporary preacher in Essex, ended with him chased out by Bishop Laud in 1630. Thereafter followed four years in the north of England, moving from position to position, one step ahead of the bishops. Along the way, he picked up a reputation as a powerful, terrifying preacher. Notes of his sermons would shortly get published, and some would become much-reprinted classics. Meanwhile, Shepard's thoughts turned increasingly to the "good land" of Massachusetts, where he imagined that he could finally "behold the face of the Lord in his Temple." The previous autumn, in 1634, his first ship had been driven back to land by storms. An infant son died in that attempt, but Shepard could not attend the funeral because Laud's agents were looking for him. The weather was bad on the second trip, the boat sprung large leaks, and his wife caught a fever from which she eventually died. Shepard never dreamed that in Massachusetts he would almost immediately find turbulence and enemies, even heretics, more extreme than he was leaving in England, and he would never acknowledge how much he contributed to creating both.

Shepard and his followers landed on October 2, 1635, and settled in Newtowne, a few miles upstream from Boston on the opposite bank of the Charles River. There Shepard's mentor and future father-in-law, the famous minister Thomas Hooker, was preparing to take his congregation to found Connecticut. Hooker, it was rumored, did not get along with Cotton, and before he left, he blasted Cotton's ideas about assurance from the pulpit.

Shepard quickly made himself a leader in the ongoing drive to tighten up the church/state disciplinary apparatus. On February 1, 1636, he founded his church at Newtowne in an elaborate ceremony that involved Shepard and six laymen making confessions of faith and giving narratives of their conversions. Magistrates and other ministers observed and signified their approval. The affair was an eloquent rebuttal of Williams's assertion of the complete independence of the churches and the state. On March 3 the General Court codified Shepard's procedure by passing an order requiring would-be churches to notify the Court and church elders. The unprecedentedly large immigration of roughly two thousand people the previous year, driven by Archbishop Laud's increasing crackdown on puritanism, swelled the colony's population by half. This surge of newcomers may have given urgency to the Court's order, as well as to its other efforts to assert its authority.

A month later, on April 1, Shepard halted the founding of Richard Mather's Dorchester church. After hearing the lay founders give conversion accounts, he questioned the men and announced to the assembly that three of them might not have had genuine conversions. Modern historians have portrayed a vigilant Shepard uncovering dangerous heresies in this episode. The historian William Hubbard, who probably knew the participants, had a less dramatic explanation for the ceremony's failure: the laypeople simply did not know what they were supposed to say about themselves in this new and intimidating ritual. Five months later, when, according to Hubbard, they had been "better informed about the nature of what was expected from them," the church was gathered without any problem. Shepard once ominously wrote of heresy hunting, "A wise shepherd had rather let a hunter come in and kill one of his sheep than let a wolf or fox escape." This was the first recorded incident in which Shepard shot at confused sheep while hunting wolves, but it would not be the last.

Around the same time that spring, Shepard began catching wind of the strange speculation circulating in Boston. It hit him hard, for a variety of reasons. Orphaned at an early age, Shepard was a desperately insecure man, with a razor-sharp mind that could all too easily get lost in labyrinths of its own creation. When he was an undergraduate, his failure to find assurance of salvation drove him to the brink of despair. Familists attracted him with promises of an experience of the Holy Spirit not dissimilar to what Cotton described. He backed off in horror at the last minute when he interpreted a passage in a book of theirs as sanctioning sinning.

The only safe path to assurance, Shepard concluded, was through hard, grueling introspective work. So strongly did he stress that path that he picked up a doctrinal quirk of his own. Puritan ministers, including Cotton, agreed that sinners could not be saved until they discovered how completely wicked and devoid of true holiness they really were. Only with this brutal preparation could they truly depend on Jesus for salvation. Yet on this topic ministers disagreed. Most argued that preparation, while necessary, was not exclusive to the elect; anything prior to justification could be experienced by the damned. Shepard, however, was part of a small group of ministers from Essex, England, including Hooker, who insisted that the preparation of the elect was intrinsically different from the experience of the damned. They might share the same dreadful terrors, but the Holy Spirit worked differently in people God intended to save. Even before justification, in other words, the hard work of piety, de-emphasized in Cotton's doctrine of assurance, was blessed by God.

Yet despite Shepard's magnification of that hard work, assurance of salvation eluded him. Looking into his own soul, he usually found no sparks of divinely implanted grace but instead endless depths of evil and self-deception. He wrote eloquently of the certainty that might come through an experience of the witness of the Spirit, whose glories were being thrown around so cheaply in Boston, but the Spirit, who could have smothered his doubts, did not speak to him.

Thus, fueled by his experience of familism, by his ambitions as a heresy hunter, and perhaps by an angry and suspicious envy, Shepard reached a momentous conclusion (in which he was certainly not alone). The rumors of strange opinions coming out of Boston indicated not simply a few otherwise sound laypeople toying with "misexpressions." A conspiracy of socially and politically powerful familist-inspired heretics threatened the colony's moral breakdown. They were being aided, perhaps intentionally, perhaps not, by Cotton's preaching. Our limited documentation suggests that Cotton had not hitherto emphasized his theological differences with his fellow ministers. Nonetheless, what was happening in Boston was so dangerous that Cotton himself, one of England's most distinguished puritans, needed to be stopped. England had seen ugly clashes and accusations of heresy between puritan ministers, but these had been restrained by the lack of puritan access to official mechanisms of repression. In Massachusetts, puritans controlled these mechanisms, the government was increasingly focusing on ideological correctness, and Shepard was already successfully taking on the role of ideological policeman.

Sometime in the spring of 1636, Shepard wrote Cotton a letter, perhaps with the encouragement of other ministers and magistrates. In that communication, the first surviving trace of the free grace controversy, he grilled Cotton on lay opinions in his congregation. His main focus, however, was a recent sermon in which Cotton preached on assurance by the immediate witness of the Spirit. Cotton's doctrine, Shepard warned, encouraged revelations. It was thus an open invitation for listeners to abandon the Bible and become familists (Cotton was preaching familist doctrine "obscurely," was how Shepard put it a decade later). Familists were more devious, Shepard cautioned, than Cotton grasped. Shepard claimed that he knew of no one holding heretical opinions in Massachusetts — he was surely fibbing at this point, for reasons that will emerge later. But he warned Cotton that someday such people might appear in his congregation, and Cotton's doctrines would allow them to do irreparable harm. "You will not thinke I have thus writ to begin or breed a quarrell," Shepard ominously ended his letter, "but to still and quiet those which are secretly begun." Shepard's implication was that Cotton must change or be responsible for spilling the secret quarrels out into the open.

Cotton responded gently but uncompromisingly to Shepard. Cotton had inquired in his congregation, and he was confident that no brethren or sisters believed in Christ any differently than he did — the most radical opinions Shepard mentioned had been offered as inquiries, and Cotton had warned against believing them. Shepard misinterpreted his sermon. Cotton was not only unaware of any quarrel between himself and his ministerial brethren; he doubted that there was any disagreement "if wee understand each other" — a polite invitation to Shepard to retreat. But Cotton did not miss the aggressive, deeply insulting undertone of Shepard's letter. He cautioned

Shepard not to compare the "faithfull practise" of Christians to familist "delusions" (Cotton had preached against familism in England), and he warned that he was not going to change his preaching in response to Shepard's doctrinal saber rattling. If Shepard wanted a fight, and events would show that he did, Cotton was willing to have it with him.

———

A fight was all the more likely to break out in 1636 because the puritan migration to Massachusetts produced a quite unanticipated stimulus to confrontation: success. In England, puritans, with their self-righteousness and severe program of social and religious reform, had always been a deeply resented minority. They expected as much, for the ungodly would always hate the godly. "Wheresoever Christ cometh, he breedeth division," as the famous puritan minister Richard Sibbes put it.

As a harassed, fighting minority, it was easy for puritans to maintain fervor. But in Massachusetts, they faced no persecution, no bishops, no large phalanx of wicked people. There was, as Shepard once put it, "no enemy to hunt you to heaven." Instead, puritans had a glut of what they thought they had always wanted: sermons, prayers, and no limits to godly companionship. The result could be a severe letdown. Many of the conversion narratives speak of a sense of spiritual disorientation and deadness upon arrival in Massachusetts. Thomas Hooker, shortly before departing for Connecticut, made a blistering attack on the godly's lack of zeal in New England, comparing it unfavorably with their attitude in England. Cotton himself worried that immigrants seemed to lose their zeal and grow complacent once they arrived. Shepard lamented that "New-Englands peace and plenty of means breed strange security."

Cotton and his congregation particularly alarmed Shepard because they appeared to be a manifestation of this problem. They were to themselves the most righteous of Protestants in the most glorious church in the world. But to Shepard, their decoupling of assurance of salvation from the effort of a constant stream of holy and pious thoughts and deeds only confirmed his larger anxiety about Massachusetts: its lack of enemies would heighten the perennial puritan danger that zeal and hard effort might wear off and be replaced by security or indifference.

There was a dangerously tempting way to compensate for the lack of enemies in Massachusetts: create them. Shepard in 1636 warned that the colony was filled with "petty Duels and jars in Churches, surmisings, censurings" because it possessed the lethal combination of "multitudes" of puritans and lack of "a common enemy to drive them together." The colony was gearing up for war in 1635 and 1636 with the Pequot Indians of southern Connecticut for reasons that have not been entirely clear either to contemporaries or to historians — the most recent chronicler of the war has accounted for it in part in terms of the puritan need for opponents.

Even if Shepard could diagnose the disease correctly, however, he had no immunity from it. The conversion narratives, whatever their other purposes, served to create a division between the saints and the rest of the world that was otherwise harder to perceive in New England than in Old. When Shepard rejected Mather's founding members, for example, he helped to preserve the ideological cohesiveness of Massachusetts, but he also helped to reassure the saints that there were still ungodly people against whom they could define themselves. Shepard once extolled the Massachusetts church admissions process as foreshadowing Christ's rejection of the damned at the Last Judgment. Cotton's church might have been a genuine menace to the peace and stability of Massachusetts, especially since ministers like Shepard had a hard time accepting disagreement of any kind. But it was also useful as an enemy for stoking zeal. If Shepard added together Cotton and his supporters, the Pequots, the church members he could berate for slackening in fervency, and those bewildered would-be Christians excluded from the churches — somewhere around half the adult population in the late 1630s — he had a rough-and-ready New World replacement, suitably dire in its own way, for the enemy-filled English social landscape that inspired puritan zeal.

Moreover, Shepard was not the only disoriented puritan to feel the appeal of making opponents. Perhaps at the same time as Shepard was intimating that Cotton preached familism, Anne Hutchinson and her allies started disseminating a no less divisive judgment: all of Massachusetts's ministers except Cotton and Wheelwright dangerously taught a covenant of works, for they told their listeners to look to their own holiness rather than to Christ for assurance of salvation. Hutchinson claimed at her trial that the minister Nathaniel Ward once said to her that Cotton's way was the "nearest way" to heaven but asked her, "Will you not acknowledge that which we hold forth to be a way too wherein we may have hope?" Had she been able to bring herself to answer yes, it is highly unlikely that Boston's hottest enemies could have rallied the forces necessary for a major, potentially self-destructive confrontation. "No truly if that be a way it is a way to hell," she replied.

Hutchinson's effect on the Boston congregation as a whole was thus probably not to induce them to embrace any of her distinctive positions. Rather, she encouraged them to perceive a critical gap between Cotton's way of finding assurance and that taught by most of Massachusetts's clergy. The errors of their neighbors only heightened their appreciation of their own church. The historian William Hubbard claimed that only a few in the Boston congregation were seriously involved in doctrinal errors. However, he also said that because of these few, "many" were inspired with a "seditious and turbulent spirit" and were "ready to challenge all, that did not run with them, to be legal [false] Christians." Cotton himself indicated as much, after things had calmed down. The resulting controversy created a refreshingly familiar stimulus to piety. As the Boston radical John Underhill told an English audience, explaining to it the necessity for conflict, even in pure churches, "Do we not ever find, the greater the afflictions and troubles of God's people be, the more eminent is his grace in the souls of his servants?"

———

Shepard's letter, ostensibly an effort to quell secret quarrels, was thus a hot spark on very dry tinder. Unfortunately, thereafter, an almost complete documentary darkness descends on Hutchinson and the free grace controversy for another half year. A single, semifictionalized anecdote from the summer of 1636 is all that survives until the end of October. If nothing else, the anecdote shows that production of enemies was well under way, and that Shepard and Hutchinson were deeply involved in their production. The layman Edward Johnson returned to Massachusetts that summer, after a five-year absence. To his surprise, he found himself in the midst of a heated conflict, which he eventually described more than a decade later in his history of New England. Johnson wrote

his account as an unabashed promoter of Massachusetts, and he suppressed any information that might create trouble for the colony.
Nevertheless, his account of his initial exposure to the controversy
has a broad ring of truth to it, if not literal accuracy.

Johnson met with some radicals after he landed — the immigrants
coming into Massachusetts usually stayed in Boston while getting ori-
ented, an obvious recipe for trouble. These radicals urged Johnson to
meet Anne Hutchinson. She surpassed the ministers in spite of all
their learning, they told him, and "admit that [the ministers] may
speake by the helpe of the spirit, yet the other goes beyond them"
(Johnson would have omitted any praise the radicals gave Cotton, who
by the time he wrote was again a respectable and important member
of the establishment; he was similarly quiet about Vane). A "little nim-
ble tongued Woman" told Johnson that Hutchinson would show him
a way, "if I could sustain it," that would fill him with such joy that he
would "never have cause to be sorry for sinne." She spoke from experience, she assured him, for she had already attained this state.

The woman's enticement came with a warning, though. "A company of legall Professors . . . lie poring on the Law . . . and when you
break it," she told Johnson, "then you breake your joy, and now no
way will serve your turne but a deepe sorrow." In other words, to be
holy was by definition to follow God's law. But if you relied on your
holiness to prove you were saved, as ministers like Shepard were
insisting, every time you broke God's commandments, you had to
panic. To call someone "legal," as she did, was to say that they were
in a covenant of works, and it was deeply insulting. Johnson had to
choose. He could rely entirely on Christ and trust to the Holy Spirit
to keep up a steady flow of bliss, as the woman promised, or he could
follow the ministers and endlessly search himself for signs of holiness,
while every time he discovered sin in himself, he must repent and
plead with God for forgiveness.

The choice between a ceaseless treadmill of guilt and anxiety and
ceaseless joy might seem an easy one. What Johnson heard, however,
only made him more anxious. That treadmill was an essential part of
his piety. He could not imagine the Christian path as anything but an
ongoing ethically based struggle: "What is the whole life of a Christian
upon this Earth?" he portrayed himself as soliloquizing upon hearing
Hutchinson and others, "But through the power of Christ to die to

sinne and live to holinesse and righteousnesse." For Johnson's nimble-tongued woman, God's "law" was a snare, but for him, it was a mirror that showed him daily his "sinfull corrupt nature" and by contrast magnified the "free grace of Christ." The renewed discovery of his own natural weakness was for Johnson the opportunity to experience the power of Christ creating holiness in him. If he could not rely on this discovery for assurance but had to depend on something as elusive as the Holy Spirit dropping the right scripture verse in his mind, he would lose the source of his comfort. The alleged "free grace" that Hutchinson and her allies offered, Johnson worried, had no transformative power; it slid through you as freely as water through a pipe. Johnson's remarks are as close as we can get to a critique by an ordinary layperson of radical Boston theology. Events suggest that he spoke for the vast majority of colonists.

But Johnson would not have known that at the time. All he knew was that he had made the perilous Atlantic crossing expecting to find a shelter from the religious storms of his native country, with puritans living together in love and agreement. Instead he discovered only more turbulence. Confused and contemplating returning to England, Johnson left Boston. He crossed the Charles River and made his way along a narrow Indian path to Newtowne. There the beating of a drum alerted him that the Thursday lecture sermon had begun. In England, magistrates, ministers, and ordinary laypeople would travel great distances together to attend the lectures of noted preachers. This custom continued in Massachusetts. Lectures were so popular that the General Court made unsuccessful attempts to limit them in 1634 and 1639, claiming that they were burdensome to ministers, audiences, and the economy. Expressing an opinion at a lecture was the fastest way a minister could disseminate it throughout the colony.

At the Newtowne meetinghouse, Shepard, "a poore weake pale complectioned man," according to Johnson, was preaching a lengthy sermon cycle he had started in June and would end four years later. The cycle consisted of a microscopically detailed exposition of Jesus' parable of the ten virgins and the bridegroom (Matthew 25:1–12). Five of the virgins were wise and truly followed the bridegroom Christ, but five were foolish and only thought they did. It was a dramatic, potentially divisive parable (who were the five foolish virgins?), and it lent itself to Shepard's urgent, combative preaching.

Shepard devoted a good deal of the cycle to attacking Boston's lay and clerical opinions. His frequently reiterated bottom line was that Boston's methods of assurance, inaccessible to him, were the refuge of false Christians. That summer Johnson might have been listening when Shepard denounced those like his nimble-tongued woman who would call devout people (like Shepard) who fasted, prayed, and mourned for their lack of grace legal Christians. Such critics dismissed the hard work of sanctification, Shepard claimed, because they had never personally felt sanctification's transforming power; they themselves were not among the saved, in other words. Shepard covered this attack with only the slightest of fig leaves: "I know not whether it be thus with any, but if I did, I would pity them."

Shepard aimed his early jabs (he would punch much harder later) not only at Boston lay radicals but at Cotton himself. He acknowledged that "very few living Christians have any settled comfortable evidence of God's eternal love to them in his Son." Nonetheless, contrary to Cotton, assurance had to come first through the evidence of holiness. Only later might people receive, if they were lucky, "an immediate witness of the Spirit of the love of Christ."

For Johnson, Shepard proved more persuasive than the radicals. He listened transformed while the hourglass was turned over twice and Shepard cleared Christ's work in the soul from "all those false Doctrines which the erronious party had afrighted him." Lest his tears should show, Johnson hung his head. By the sermon's end, Shepard had a foot soldier; Johnson was ready "to live and die with the Ministers of New England."

The documentary trail of Hutchinson and the free grace controversy picks up again at the end of October 1636, with the last effort to keep the quarrels contained. On October 25, Shepard and six other ministers gathered in John Cotton's parlor. Meeting with them were Cotton, pastor Wilson, ruling lay elder Thomas Leverett, and deacon John Coggeshall, along with Hutchinson's brother-in-law John Wheelwright.

Wheelwright had arrived in May, joined the Boston church, and was preaching informally in an outlying Boston settlement, Mount Wollaston. His theology was fundamentally the same as Cotton's: they both held that assurance of salvation first had to come through the Holy Spirit revealing an absolute promise of salvation (thus separating them from most ministers); however, they insisted that conversion created a real transformation in believers (thus separating them from most radicals, who argued (or speculated) that in conversion, the divine simply obliterated the earthly). But Wheelwright was unlike Cotton in that he used more reckless terminology and did not back away from fights. He was also unlike Cotton in that most ministers would not have known much about him except that he was Anne Hutchinson's brother-in-law, which was not a reassuring credential.

The Bostonians listened carefully, as some of the ministers explained that they had come to warn the Boston church of the danger it was in, and to press upon it the difficulties that it was making for the other churches. Wheelwright was delivering strange doctrines in his sermons, some claimed. What exactly did Cotton believe? What were they doing about Anne Hutchinson? Cotton and Wheelwright both explained that they believed that sanctification could help reinforce assurance, and the ministers had a discussion about how the Holy Spirit dwelled in believers, on which there were a variety of opinions.

When the conversation turned to Hutchinson, it got heated. Ministers told Cotton that rumors were circulating that their preaching, unlike Cotton's, was "not according to the gospel." As far as they could determine, Hutchinson was instrumental in spreading those rumors. The General Court was in session down the street, and some minister, clearly frustrated with the talk, said they should go there to voice their concerns. That way (taking church quarrels precipitously to the state) would not be according to God, Cotton replied, and they decided to call Hutchinson.

Hutchinson came and, after much urging from the ministers, gave them a guarded glimpse of her opinion of them. They were not able ministers of the New Testament. Their problem, she explained, was that they mistakenly preached the seal of the Spirit on a work — they taught, in other words, that people could take assurance of salvation from their holiness, not from a scripture revelation of God's love. They were like the apostles before Christ's Resurrection and Ascension. Their preaching showed that they had not yet been properly sealed with the Spirit; that only happened to the apostles when the

Holy Spirit descended in tongues of fire on them at Pentecost after Christ had ascended to heaven. Shepard had not been sealed, she informed him, because he preached that love could be evidence of justification.

Some persons present, including Cotton and the ruling elder, Thomas Leverett, and even perhaps some of the other ministers, did not hear her saying anything horribly shocking. Being compared to Christ's disciples was not on the face of it the worst thing a minister could have said about him. Cotton and Leverett understood her to be saying that the ministers were decent preachers but not as developed as Cotton because they had not yet experienced the Holy Spirit in its full force. Moreover, some ministers were probably more capable than others of shrugging off what might have seemed maladroit, even silly, observations by an untrained and presumptuously judgmental woman — one minister whom Hutchinson did not know mischievously led her on to tell him that he was not yet properly sealed with the Spirit.

But there was good reason to suspect Hutchinson's words, for a comparison between her and the pre-Resurrection apostles was even more derogatory than she indicated to them. As would come out later, Hutchinson believed that it was only after Christ's death that the apostles had been truly converted to the covenant of grace. Like the unconverted apostles, the preachers of Massachusetts, with their talk of self-examination for holiness, stood teetering on the brink of hell (hence Hutchinson's warning to Ward about where he was taking his listeners). The only thing that distinguished an unconverted apostle from a disciple of Antichrist was that the former did not persecute true Christians. But if the ministers persisted in harassing those like Hutchinson who truly understood the meaning of Christ's Resurrection and Ascension, then that distinction no longer held for them, and they were the enemies of the saints.

No need, though, for Hutchinson to go into all these nuances to an unsympathetic audience. Cotton told her it was regrettable that she made comparisons between the ministers. However, still in his no-disagreements-if-we-understand-each-other mode, he told the ministers that all Hutchinson meant was that "you did hold forth some matter in your preaching that was not pertinent to the seal of the spirit." He heard nothing warranting the negative reactions of some ministers. When Hutchinson was out of Cotton's earshot at the meeting, she told Nathaniel Ward that their preaching was a path to hell. One can picture Ward later going back to Cotton, and Cotton finding himself in an impossible he-said, she-said situation. Since Cotton admired Hutchinson and by now had his own back up from the belligerence and hostility of ministers like Shepard, he would have given her the benefit of the doubt, not for the first or last time.

Shepard was sharp enough, however, and perhaps stung enough, to sense that Hutchinson had not put all her cards on the table. The pre-pentecostal disciples were saved, he shortly thereafter insisted from the pulpit: "Tho' they were not as yet sealed, yet they knew . . . that Christ was their's." Hutchinson's dissembling only confirmed his long-standing intuition that some ghastly secretive heresy lurked in Boston. As he wrote to John Winthrop a few months later, the town had "hidden misteries" that he was certain would eventually emerge. He was right, but the mysteries were not of the magnitude that he imagined, and a major reason why the controversy would spiral out of control was that he and his allies repeatedly and aggressively fingered the wrong suspects for the wrong crimes.

Wheelwright was the chief object of their overreaction. Shortly before the October meeting, he had preached a sermon in which he portrayed the union of Christ and the Holy Spirit with believers in unusually intimate terms. Such a portrayal was extremely rare, although not completely unheard of, from orthodox ministers. An unsympathetic listener (we do not know whom) decided that Wheelwright gave such an intimate depiction in order to hint at a conviction that he dared not express openly: in conversion, a believer was not transformed by God but united with him and became "God-man, even Jesus Christ" — pure familist doctrine. Familists were notorious for their willingness to fib about their beliefs, and Wheelwright had presented his real convictions as openly as one could expect.

Once it had been decided that Wheelwright covertly taught familist doctrine, corroborating evidence came tumbling in. After the October meeting, some ministers recalled that Wheelwright there answered pointed questions from Shepard in a way that indicated that he had a familist conception of the witness of the Spirit. Wheelwright hotly denied the accuracy of the ministers' memories, as did others from Boston who were present. It may not be a coincidence that Shepard himself had the clearest hostile memory of the exchange. Perhaps the other ministers had the significance and details of the exchange clarified (or created) for them by Shepard.

––––––

Cotton later claimed that a number of the ministers left the meeting satisfied. They told him they would no longer listen to rumors and that the topic was closed. But some of those ministers subsequently informed him that they were less satisfied than before. One might picture Shepard and the other militants among them explaining what they had just heard. Slippery though Hutchinson might have been and reluctant to speak in the first place, she made it clear that she had little respect for the ministers, to say no worse. Wheelwright, for some ministers, had confirmed that he was a discreet familist. Moreover, any hopes that those ministers might have had that the Boston church would take seriously their concerns about their reputations and Boston's dangerous ideas must have been severely weakened by the conduct of the Boston elders present. Cotton seemed incapable of hearing any serious disagreement in the room. Nor did Leverett find anything offensive in Hutchinson's observations. This was not an eldership poised for disciplinary action to deal with what at least some ministers were starting to see as a major policing problem. If enemies could not be tackled privately, then the next step for ministers like Shepard and his allies would be to tackle them openly. The secret quarrels would become public, as Shepard six months previously had warned Cotton would happen.

CHAPTER 4

Antichristian Spirits and Soul Robbers

Fall–Winter 1636–1637

As the autumn of 1636 drew to a close, the free grace controversy reached a turning point. Previously, its issues had been ventilated in informal encounters among laypeople, in ministers' parlors, and in brief pulpit remarks by a few militant clergy. In the late fall and winter, they were aired with growing vehemence in crowded meetinghouses, in the General Court, and in prolonged pulpit tirades. Debates turned to confrontations, and participants increasingly failed to see their opponents as brethren and sisters who had been driven across the Atlantic in a holy common cause. Rather, they were enemies of that cause, participants in Satan's ages-long plot to destroy Christianity. He was making impressive strides at pushing back the Reformation in England, while in Germany his Roman Catholic tools were devastating the Protestants in the Thirty Years' War. Now in Massachusetts, his fifth column was blasting a breach through the walls of discipline that protected its pure churches.

———

Five days after the October meeting, an open confrontation in the Boston church broke out. Someone convinced of Wheelwright's familist tendencies had worked hard and successfully on Deputy Governor Winthrop to make sure that he saw them. The task had been urgent. The previous Sunday, October 23, two days before the ministerial conference, the residents of Mount Wollaston, where Wheelwright preached, petitioned the Boston church to have him made a teacher in the church along with Cotton. Their request was to come up the following Sunday for resolution. Mount Wollaston, part of Boston, was a cumbersome ten miles and more from the Boston meetinghouse. A number of settlers, including the Hutchinsons and others who were to become deeply involved in the free grace controversy, had farms there. Its inhabitants had been trying to get permission to form their own church and town since the summer, but with no success. The Bostonians worried that the loss of Mount Wollaston and its taxes would hurt Boston's prosperity. Were Wheelwright officially made a minister to the Boston congregation, he could immediately administer the sacraments at Mount Wollaston.

————

If the absence of comments in Winthrop's journal about the free grace controversy up to this point is any gauge of his attitude, he had been slow to perceive its seriousness. A number of reasons might account for this. He admired Cotton greatly, and, unlike Shepard, he himself had experienced the witness of the Spirit. Both of these factors might have made him more hesitant than others to hear serious heresy within the Boston congregation. Winthrop was also more tolerant and patient than Massachusetts's most severe leaders. Nonetheless, by the end of October, his level of concern was rising. We know from his journal that he now considered Hutchinson a divisive influence in the community with dangerous opinions, and the argument about Wheelwright's familism hit home with him, perhaps in part because Winthrop's family had long been friends with the minister John Knewstub, an ancient enemy of the Family of Love.

On Sunday, October 30, a newly alarmed Winthrop arose from the magistrate's bench with two objections to Wheelwright's appointment. The church was already well supplied with ministers, he said, and Wheelwright's sermon on union with Christ showed that his doctrine was questionable. Wheelwright seemed to dissent in judgment from the church, Winthrop concluded — a polite way of saying that he reeked of familism. When challenged by Vane and Wheelwright, Winthrop refused to back down. He could not consent to his appointment to the Boston church. The church allowed Winthrop to block Wheelwright on the understanding that the formation of a new church at Mount Wollaston would move forward (it is probably not coincidental, however, that the creation of a church and town at Mount Wollaston was delayed until two years after the General Court banished Wheelwright).

Winthrop's attack on Wheelwright, besides thwarting the will of most of the Boston congregation, crossed a boundary that our sources suggest had been hitherto honored — do not attack anyone by name, at least when speaking in public or to people you did not know and trust. Shepard hitherto ostentatiously maintained in the pulpit that he did not know if anyone in Massachusetts held the opinions he savaged so fiercely. Johnson's nimble-tongued woman told him that the ministers preached with the aid of the spirit. Hutchinson shared her opinions about the ministers only after a great deal of persuasion. There were two reasons for this restraint. One was that insulting people was potentially a criminal offense. The second, more immediately applicable reason was that the saints were supposed to love, not attack, each other, and every church member in Massachusetts was a certified saint. If you had disagreements with a saint, you went first to them; if you received no satisfaction, you took your complaint to the church elders, who launched their own investigation. What you did not do was what Winthrop had just done: lob charges with no warning at important public meetings.

Thus it was understandable that Winthrop's behavior offended other members of the congregation, as he acknowledged in his journal. Coming from a less important member, it might have received an official rebuke. It was also in keeping with his authoritarian character. Winthrop, a humorless, austere man, was widely admired for his rectitude, good judgment, and devotion to the colony. However, he had not been reelected governor for the last three years, in part because as governor in 1634 he had tried to stall when the freemen demanded the full legislative powers allowed them in the colony's charter and in part because of his refusal to bind his conduct to procedural norms.

The next day Winthrop defended himself in another speech before the congregation, perhaps in a special meeting called to discuss his actions. He told the congregation that he now had spoken privately with Wheelwright. Though Wheelwright denied holding the views he was accused of, he nevertheless held them by necessary consequence. "Necessary consequence" meant that even if Wheelwright did not say exactly what Winthrop accused him of meaning, Winthrop could deduce that meaning from what he said, and therefore he meant it. There was no room to challenge Winthrop's judgment on Wheelwright, since it did not depend directly on Wheelwright's words. When Winthrop finished, no one answered him.

That silence should not be mistaken for consent. "The *Bostoners in N[ew] E[ngland]*. . . . would have chosen Mr *Wheelwright* (the notorious Familist) to have been co-teacher with Mr C[otton] there, had not some few withstood it," is how this incident was explained to an English minister. But where Winthrop may have seen a familist and a clerical traitor, Cotton saw an orthodox minister, by his standards, and there is no reason to think that most of his congregation would not have agreed. Winthrop's heavy-handed intervention, instead of waking the congregation up to the dangerous nature of the theological inquiries in Hutchinson's circle, provided the radicals with cover and made more plausible to a wider group, including Cotton, the Hutchinsonian depiction of ministers and magistrates lost in an anti-Christian covenant of works.

———

Thereafter, the mutual intolerance rapidly mounted. Shepard escalated the harshness of his pulpit attacks, even asserting that Cotton's doctrines would lead to the Bible being abandoned. If you could make the Bible tell you that you personally were saved, Shepard argued, you could make it say anything, which was one step away from abandoning it. Cotton later claimed that the severity of the attacks on him made him less inclined to believe what was said about people like Hutchinson.

In December Cotton and an unknown number of ministers exchanged letters on the topic of assurance. The letters, which circulated among the laity, grew increasingly ill-tempered. The ministers told Cotton that his teaching encouraged sin, destroyed the hope of insecure Christians, and encouraged listeners to forsake the scriptures. Cotton denied that his teachings would have any such ill effect and declared his solidarity with the laity in his congregation. An angry Cotton had already decided that the extreme preparationism of Shepard and Hooker amounted to Roman Catholic salvation through works. Now he warned his opponents that even to say that sanctification could give a first assurance of salvation smelled of Catholicism.

Laity fared no better in their attempts to talk out their differences. Some of the laity of Shepard's Newtowne congregation met for a conference with laity from Boston in December. We know of the conference from an angry paper that the Bostonians wrote shortly thereafter.

In that document, the Bostonians complained that Shepard's laypeople had taken their positions, all derived from Cotton's teachings, and twisted them out of shape to turn them into heresies. The Newtowne men not only distorted the Bostonians' doctrines but also signaled forcefully that they had given up on finding church solutions to their quarrels. With no warning, the Bostonians complained, they handed their version of the conference over to the General Court.

———

But the General Court meeting in December proved as polarized on this issue as the churches. When the Court convened in the Boston meetinghouse, Governor Vane sprang the news that he was leaving the colony — on family business, he first claimed. When pressed, he added that he would not have considered leaving except for two reasons: he feared that God's wrath would descend on the colony for its disputes, and he deeply resented the gossip circulating (with a good deal of truth to it) that he was the cause of those disturbances. Therefore, he thought it best that he step down for a time. His decision was an unpopular one, and the Boston church met and decided not to release him. By the rigorous standards of community that these saints were trying to maintain, you could not leave your church unless the church gave its consent.

After Vane had calmed down, the Court called the ministers for advice. The ministers started arguing over whether sanctification could be a first evidence of justification. Cotton insisted no, and all the other ministers argued yes. Wheelwright sat by, listening and drawing his own conclusions, which he would shortly broadcast spectacularly from the pulpit. Wilson made a speech denouncing the radicals' practice of charging that opponents were under a covenant of works. He linked this practice to theological delusion, to advocating a "false Covenant and a fancy[i.e., imaginary]-Christ." Wilson warned of a possible separation if the differences were not healed, perhaps a reference to the Mount Wollaston situation. Most of the magistrates and all the ministers but Wheelwright and Cotton seconded Wilson. Vane and the new Salem minister Hugh Peters got into a clash in which Peters blamed the current unrest in Massachusetts on Vane. Vane replied that the gospel always brought strife and that those under a covenant of works (like Peters) would always persecute the saints. Peters retorted that Vane was young, inexperienced, and given to peremptory conclusions, and that, from Peters's experience, the causes of theological opinions like his were pride, idleness, and ungrounded knowledge.

With ministers and magistrates verbally at each other's throats, the Court decided to appeal to the only source of help left it. It passed a motion calling for the churches to beseech God for aid in a day of fasting and humiliation on January 19. Reasons for the fast also included the "miserable estate of the churches in Germany" and "the bishops [in England] making havock in the churches, putting down the faithful ministers, and advancing popish ceremonies and doctrines." Massachusetts's troubles were part of a larger crisis of Protestantism.

———

Two weeks later, the Boston meetinghouse was the scene of the oddest event of December, the informal Boston church disciplining not of Hutchinson or any other radical, but of pastor Wilson. New England's early historians were consistent in their praises of Wilson, all admiring his extraordinary humility and his great charity "where there was any sign and hopes of good." Although he was conventional in his theology, as far as anyone can tell, he and Cotton got along well in their nearly two decades of working together, except for this one episode. Wilson had left for England to fetch his wife, Elizabeth, shortly after Hutchinson arrived and returned on the same ship as Shepard. Once back, according to Cotton, he went for a long time without viewing anything as seriously amiss in the congregation until in a conference his wife had arranged with a radical, the radical spoke freely about his or her views. Wilson first publicly criticized the radicals in his December speech in the Court.

In that speech Wilson had not specified the new opinions he found dangerous, but the church called him to defend himself on December 31. He told the church that he did not mean doctrines delivered by Cotton and Wheelwright. By now Cotton had been so burned by attacks from ministers like Shepard that he refused to believe Wilson. Most of the church, including Cotton, wanted to give Wilson an admonition, but Winthrop and one or two others blocked them (the Boston church attempted to make decisions by consensus). Instead, Cotton gave him a grave exhortation.

Wilson preached the next day to the general satisfaction of the congregation, however. Vane himself publicly approved. Would that we knew what the contents of this sermon were; its reception indicates that lines within the Boston church were not yet entirely hardened, despite the mutual provocation.

―――――

Nonetheless, by January, the pulpits of Massachusetts were too often being used to slash, not heal. In 1645, Shepard wrote that after the clerical conferences with Cotton failed to produce an understanding, ministers began publicly denouncing Boston doctrines, lay and ministerial, for the first time. Shepard's chronology was disingenuous — he had been denouncing Boston doctrines from the pulpit for at least half a year before the failure of those conferences. But his statement acknowledges a rise in the heat of pulpit rhetoric. Winthrop noted at the end of January that "the ministers of both sides . . . did publicly declare their judgments . . . so as all men's mouths were full of them."

The most famous of those slashing sermons took place on January 19, 1637, the General Court's fast day. All across the colony that morning the saints made their way to their rough, unheated meetinghouses, prepared for a frigid day of sermons, psalm singing, and prayer. In their meetinghouses, they were to lament the dissensions in their colony and beseech God to aid them. The night before, those saints who were rigorously following puritan prescriptions for fasting would have stinted on food and sleep, and ministers advised even newlyweds to abstain from sex. On the fast day itself, dressed in their plainest and cheapest apparel to show their humility and self-abasement, they would be feeling the pinch of lack of nourishment, and they would have come to the daylong services well loaded with coins to give for alms.

Fasting for the purposes of knowing God's intentions behind some calamity and averting his continued anger was one of the institutional practices of the Church of England. Puritans fasted enthusiastically in pursuit of their political goals, and as a result, fasts unauthorized by a bishop were banned in 1604. The ban hardly stopped puritans from fasting. One of Winthrop's English correspondents wrote him in 1636 that fasts were now looked upon "as hateful as conventicles," yet had it not been for "the private prayers and fastes of many of Gods deare Servants," famine would have stalked England that year as divine punishment for the policies of Archbishop Laud. Fasting was also a weapon in the arsenal of the saints: in 1630 God struck dead the persecuting archbishop of York, Samuel Harsnett, on the very day when a group of puritan ministers fasted against him.

In Boston on the General Court's fast day, Cotton preached in the morning and Wheelwright was asked to speak in the afternoon. Why fast? Wheelwright began the sermon that was to get him banished from Massachusetts. Not in the first instance for temporal blessings, nor to avert domestic and foreign evils (as the General Court had requested); that was why heathens and hypocrites fasted. Genuine Christians, however, fasted only because of the absence of Christ; have Christ, and all blessings followed. Thus, in order to accomplish the Court's goals in a truly Christian way, Wheelwright's audience had to desire the presence of Christ among them.

Having corrected the General Court on the nature of a true Christian fast, Wheelwright explained what hindered the presence of Christ in Massachusetts. It was Antichrist, working through his antichristian spirits. Those spirits propagated a covenant of works wherever they could and introduced a false Christ in place of the real one. A dead giveaway to their identity was that they taught that sanctification could be a first evidence of justification. Wheelwright followed the conventional etiquette of naming no names, but his audience surely knew that almost all the ministers in Massachusetts fit this description.

Another characteristic of antichristian spirits was that they invariably persecuted the saints (perhaps Wheelwright had Winthrop's blackball in mind as he spoke this). Moreover, those spirits would win unless the saints fought back. Therefore, to keep Christ in Massachusetts, Wheelwright's audience had to fight a spiritual combat and kill their opponents with the word of the Lord. If necessary, they would die like sheep, confident that their glorious martyrdoms would have more effect than their lives. Christ wanted his church purged, and in any case, it was impossible to preach the gospel correctly and maintain peace and quiet.

Wheelwright then imagined "objections" to his doctrine and answered them. One of these objections was that Wheelwright's call for spiritual combat would cause a combustion in the church and commonwealth. Wheelwright replied, "I confess and acknowledge it will do so, but what then?" The stakes were enormous, he explained. If

Antichrist were defeated, then the Jews would be converted and the church would enter its millennial period of prosperity and peace before the return of Christ.

Wheelwright ended this visionary and bitterly uncharitable sermon by affirming that his party were the true friends of Church and Commonwealth. They were trying to bring in Christ, and if Christ was present, there would be no more need for fasting. His opponents, on the other hand, since they deludedly fasted in the first instance to seek blessings and remove evils, went in opposition to the ways of Christ. They were "the greatest enimyes to the state that can be."

While historians portray Wheelwright's conviction for this call to arms as almost inevitable, he was hardly alone in his slash-and-burn rhetoric. The preaching of most ministers has not survived, but we can listen in on Shepard, for his sermons from this period were preserved and later published. Satan "will follow Christ into the wilderness," he told his listeners sometime that winter, for "he seeks to make his party within the Church." Satan would make that party, Shepard warned, through the agency of the Jesuits. The Jesuits were a recently formed Roman Catholic order dedicated to driving back the Reformation, and Protestants widely feared them as spies and secret agents. One of the most subtle tricks of the Jesuits, Shepard cautioned his audience, was not to oppose Protestantism directly but to set Protestants fighting one another.

Who might be the dupes of Satan and the Jesuits in Massachusetts, and why had they been so hard to detect? They were, Shepard announced, "evangelical hypocrites." They were frauds, but almost unidentifiable because they acted so convincingly pious. Like the best Protestants, they denied that they could be saved by their own efforts, and they threw themselves upon Christ for salvation and rejoiced. But they rejoiced not because they felt the gospel invigorating them in the battle against sin but because they mistakenly believed that they no longer had to worry about that battle. Thereafter, the hypocrites denied the need for holiness altogether and cried up, "Grace only." The delusion of the evangelical hypocrites that they were saved made them the perfect destructive tools of Satan, and they would wake from their delusion only in hell. Like Wheelwright, Shepard named no names, but it is hard to imagine that anyone in his audience failed to guess who had prompted his terminology.

Satan, however, was not the ultimate supernatural agent stirring Massachusetts's evangelical hypocrites into action; it was God himself, ultimate cause of everything that happened. Shepard reminded his audience that when God unleashed the Thirty Years' War against the German Protestants, many of them reverted to Catholicism. In England, hypocrites who had previously rejoiced in puritanism were crumbling under Archbishop Laud's attack. Some of these hypocrites instead fled to Massachusetts, and to catch them, the Lord unleashed doctrinal error, and they fell. Thus, God was the ultimate source of Protestantism's recent troubles, working with a ruthless fury to expose false Protestants everywhere. "God is trying all his Friends through all the christian world," Shepard explained, and most of those friends were proving false.

Shepard therefore was not only revealing Jesuit plots when he attacked Boston, and he was not only defending the Massachusetts front in a pan-European religious war. Shepard was participating in God's geographically sweeping, violent exposure of Protestant hypocrites. With that divine authority behind him, he launched his most sustained and overt attack on Boston to date. He claimed, just as he had done when writing to Cotton to accuse him of heresy many months previously, that he spoke only in the interest of peace: "I will only speak . . . not to begin, but if possible to still division."

Shepard's way of stilling divisions remained exactly as it had been when he wrote his letter to Cotton the previous spring. Virtually all the members of the Boston church, from the most zealous lay radical to Cotton, had to concede they were wrong. Shepard warned his audience of the danger of a wide variety of propositions advanced by radicals or by Cotton that denigrated God's grace. Those propositions served to "trample under-foot Christ's blood," and unless Shepard's opponents repented, for them was "reserved the very blackness of darkness forever." It is hard to imagine that most ministers were in as unrestrained an attack mode as Shepard, but it is easy to imagine that his Thursday lecture sermon listeners from Boston did not take kindly to hearing from him that they were damned and controlled by Jesuit agents or that they were "the worms that grow in this wood, in this building, in these churches."

By the winter, even the mild Cotton had been pushed into pulpit slashing, in his restrained way. He warned that those who listened to his opponents' preaching would not discover Christ and risked damnation. In one of his sermons, he allegedly said that the difference between him and his opponents was as great as that between heaven and hell.

Boston laity picked up on the aggression of their ministers. In February, Winthrop noted in his journal that members of what he called "Mr. Cotton's party" were attending the lectures of other ministers and "did make much disturbance by public questions, and objections to their doctrines, which did any way disagree from their opinions." The minister Thomas Weld compared the questions to "halfe a dozen Pistols discharged at the face of the Preacher." The ministers, according to Weld, were called "Legall Preachers, Baal's Priests, Popish Factors, Scribes, Pharisees, and Opposers of Christ himselfe." Winthrop claimed that "it began to be as common here to distinguish between men, by being under a covenant of grace or a covenant of works, as in other countries between Protestants and papists." According to Boston church member Giles Firmin, Henry Vane was particularly active in challenging ministers' doctrine. He "was the man that did embolden them, when ministers had done preaching, he would find questions to put to them, though they were strangers." Cotton later claimed that Wheelwright's fast-day rhetoric encouraged the boldness of the radicals, but he also acknowledged that his and Wheelwright's supporters participated in the questioning.

———

It is the Bostonians' aggression that scholars tend to notice, understandably, since their opponents wrote the most accessible accounts of the free grace controversy. But that one-sided picture misses the stark polarization into which the controversy had descended by the winter. Weld inadvertently alluded to the other side when he acknowledged that Cotton's party did not discharge their pistols at random. They fired when "they heard a Minister was upon such a point as was like to strike at their opinions, with a purpose to oppose him to his face." We know now from Shepard's example that the Massachusetts establishment was not averse to discharging pistols in the face of its opponents, and aggression often probably lay in the eye of the beholder. Weld himself reportedly made violent attacks on Boston, and his church appears to have been the most conflicted church outside

Boston. Weld noted disapprovingly that radicals walked out of the Boston meetinghouse whenever Wilson preached; these were women led by Hutchinson, Winthrop claimed. What Weld and Winthrop failed to mention was that Wilson was also forbidding anyone in his household to attend conventicles at Hutchinson's house, warning that "whatsoever they may pretend, they will rob you of ordinances, rob you of your souls, rob you of your God." There was now loud agreement that false saints were handing out false road maps to heaven in Massachusetts's godly commonwealth, but there was no agreement about who those false saints were.

CHAPTER 5

A Combustion in the Commonwealth

Spring 1637

As accusations of Jesuit dupes and antichristian spirits openly flew around, it was inevitable that some participants would move from attempting to persuade their opponents to attempting to coerce them. Since Cotton's party was heavily outnumbered, it was also inevitable that it would be opponents of him and his allies who would find coercion attractive. Massachusetts's congregational churches had no power to coerce each other. Coercion could come only from the state, and thus in the spring of 1637, the free grace controversy metamorphosed into a political dispute. The transformation, however, only made it all the more difficult to resolve.

Wheelwright became the first object of coercion. He was an obvious target, Hutchinson's relative and without Cotton's prestige, and on the fast day he had broadcast inflammatory arguments that certainly seemed aimed at most of the ministers in Massachusetts. But creating a secular legal issue of his sermon was not simple. Godly ministers heaping abuse on each other's doctrines was, on the face of it, a church issue, not a state one. However, if it could be demonstrated that Wheelwright was not godly, but a heretic, then the law might come into play. A heretic preaching his doctrine was, by definition, trying to turn other people into heretics. Moreover, when that heretic called his opponents antichristian and urged his party of heretics to cause a combustion in the commonwealth, his preaching obviously threatened the public good and was clearly seditious (disruptive of public authority). As such, it was no longer the sole concern of the churches but fell within the jurisdiction of the General Court. The problem with Wheelwright's fast-day sermon for this line of reasoning was that however abrasive it might have been, it was not obviously heretical.

Wheelwright himself offered a way out of that problem. Unfriendly listeners were attending his preaching at Mount Wollaston, which did not cause him to moderate it. In one sermon, he announced that faith and repentance were no parts of the covenant of grace. Believing belonged to the damnable covenant of works, he was said to have claimed. What he meant was that people could fool themselves that any belief, faith, or repentance they might feel came from God's grace, when in fact those sentiments had been their own creation. God had to first tell them through the witness of the Spirit that they were saved before they could trust such signs. That is how he later explained himself, and had he been a more temperate man, he would have expressed himself more carefully. But since he did not, it was easy to take him to have argued that people could assure that they were saved even if they did not have faith in Christ or repentance for their sins. Moral chaos would obviously result from such heretical teaching.

Hostile ministers seized upon this sermon to initiate the pivotal trial of the free grace controversy. In the winter of 1637, they secretly presented a list of doctrinal charges against Wheelwright, drawn mostly from the Mount Wollaston sermon, to the General Court. Perhaps feeling guilty about their underhanded tactics, they insisted that they wrote not to aggravate Wheelwright's fault in the eye of authority but to convince him of his error and bring him to repent (but why did they not come to me first, Wheelwright complained later, failing to add that it would have made no impact on him had they done so). They introduced their solicitude for Wheelwright, he claimed, with "many bitter invectives, ranking me amongst the instruments of Satan, acted by him, to pull down the Kingdom of Christ upon earth, because I could not do it in heaven, &c."

The General Court, armed with this accusation, gathered in the Boston meetinghouse on March 9, ready to assume the judicial role it shared with its legislative and executive duties. As a judicial body, the Court's members, twelve magistrates (the governor, deputy governor, and the assistants) and thirty-three town deputies, interchangeably acted as prosecutors, judges, jury, and, to a much lesser extent, defense advocates. Vane, as governor, was chief presiding officer, but he seems to have had little control over this session, perhaps due to his lack of experience at political hardball. It was deputies who asked that Wheelwright be sent for because of his fast-day sermon; in the usually overlooked excerpts from the trial published by "S.G." in 1676, deputies William Spencer from Newtowne, Shepard's congregant, and Richard Collicot of Dorchester are Wheelwright's most aggressive pursuers.

Winthrop later wrote in an "Apology" defending the Court's action. In it, he claimed that the move to examine Wheelwright came simply because Wheelwright's fast-day sermon tended to "sedition, and disturbance of the publicke peace." His claim, however, was a covering-of-tracks maneuver, done deftly enough that both it and the element of the trial it was intended to obscure have evaded notice by historians. The deputies' actual accusation charged Wheelwright with "preaching on the Fast Day a *Heretical* [my italics] and Seditious Sermon, tending to Mutiny and Disturbance." The exact wording of the charge was important; Wheelwright's prosecutors intended to make heresy a major excuse for crossing the sensitive boundary between church and state; if heresy was not present, then they were left with the delicate task of demonstrating on other grounds that a sermon whose doctrine was similar to Cotton's and which had been approved by the colony's governor justified the extreme step of state prosecution. The Court assented to the deputies' request, and Wheelwright was notified to be ready to appear in the next two or three days.

The next maneuver of Wheelright's opponents also went smoothly. The Court fined Stephen Greensmith, a Boston lumber dealer, for saying with more recklessness than theological acuity that all the ministers in the colony except Wheelwright, Cotton, and, "hee thought," Thomas Hooker (the minister most opposed to them), were under a covenant of works. It ordered Greensmith, for good measure, to apologize in every church. Overtly slander the ministers, and this Court had no reluctance to punish you.

Yet that conviction hardly means that the Court was stacked against Wheelwright. We know nothing of the details of the Greensmith hearing, but his greatest crime might have been naming names to people who got offended. Conceivably, had a member of Shepard's congregation told the wrong audience that Wheelwright and Cotton were soul-damning familists, he or she might have found themselves in front of the Court.

The limits of the Court's prosecutorial zeal were exposed by the next item on its agenda. According to Winthrop, the Court, meaning the self-appointed prosecutors, "questioned the proceeding against Mr. Wilson [when the Boston church informally disciplined Wilson after his speech in the General Court the previous December]." The prosecutors wanted to "fasten upon such as had prejudiced him." This attempt to second-guess a church disciplinary proceeding got nowhere. A majority of the Court voted to approve Wilson's speech, but it was not willing to break the barrier between the churches and the state and question the Boston church's action. In fact, the assistant William Coddington, a Wheelwright supporter, later claimed that a majority of the assistants were not predisposed to punishing Wheelwright. That claim is entirely possible. Three of them, Governor Vane, Coddington, and Richard Dummer, were Wheelwright's partisans, and four other assistants, John Humphrey, Simon Bradstreet, Richard Bellingham, and John Winthrop Jr., in the years to come on occasion showed more tolerance of religious diversity than many of their fellow magistrates.

Winthrop and his allies, however, had not finished strengthening their hand for Wheelwright's trial. They called in the ministers for advice about the Court's authority in church issues. There surely had been some presession planning going on, because when the ministers came in, they agreed upon two things, both of which were highly advantageous to the prosecution of Wheelwright. (But what did they not agree on? What were the debates that led up to this agreement? Does the pronoun "all" really cover Cotton? Winthrop does not tell us.) First, the separation of church and state meant that Court members could not be questioned in their churches regarding their speeches in the Court. Winthrop therefore could not be disciplined in his church for anything he did in this Court. Second, the ministers concluded that the state could take disciplinary action against a church member before his or her church had done so "in all such heresies or errors of any church member as are manifest and dangerous to the state." That conclusion gave a ministerial green light to the prosecution of Wheelwright for the spiritual crime of heresy, even though the Boston church had not tried him for it.

Having laid the groundwork for Wheelwright's conviction, the Court summoned him. Our knowledge of Wheelwright's trial comes mostly from Winthrop's "Apology," which was scarcely a disinterested document. Winthrop, however, wrote for a local audience, aware that records of the trial taken in shorthand by Wheelwright's friends were circulating. Thus, he probably did not state anything overtly incorrect, but, as will be seen, he was careful about what he chose to present and how he presented it. Wheelwright gave the Court a copy of his sermon, and he was dismissed until the next day.

Wheelwright was called in the next morning for a private session thick with mutual distrust. Wheelwright wanted to know who his accusers were (English defendants at this time were not told in advance what the evidence against them was, nor were they allowed legal counsel). Someone answered that the copy of the sermon he gave the Court was his accuser, and since he had acknowledged it to be his, the court might proceed ex officio. The reply could be taken to mean, and perhaps was intended to mean, that Wheelwright, through his sermon, had incriminated himself. In England, the hated ecclesiastical Court of High Commission had made puritan ministers accuse themselves through a self-incriminating ex officio oath. According to Winthrop, "great exception was taken, as if the Court intended the course of the High Commission." Someone nimbly stepped in and claimed that all the term meant was that the Court acted by authority.

Wheelwright's friends on the Court calmed him down, but the next question set the room in an uproar again. Did Wheelwright know when he preached his sermon that most ministers in the country taught what he called a covenant of works? Saying yes would have been an acknowledgment that Wheelwright had tried to criminally incite his listeners to form a party against them. He sensibly refused to answer. Wheelwright's supporters on the Court protested that the prosecutors were trying to ensnare Wheelwright and that the question had nothing to do with the contents of the sermon. Since Wheelwright refused to convict himself, the closed morning session ended in a stalemate.

In the afternoon, the Court requested that the ministers be present for advice. Having opened its doors to the ministers, it decided to let in the general public as well, which resulted in the Boston meetinghouse being packed. Wheelwright was again asked if he had meant that any of the ministers or Christians in the churches of Massachusetts "walked" under a covenant of works. He carefully replied that if any walked in such a fashion, they were whom he meant. Wheelwright's enemies had gotten nowhere in attempting to force him to incriminate himself.

Since Wheelwright was not going to convict himself of seditious speech, the prosecution brought up the Mount Wollaston sermon to prove the heresy charge. Wheelwright, in response, explained to the Court his extremely complicated conception of the place of faith and repentance in the covenant of grace. If you were a professional theologian, you might find much in the convolutions of Wheelwright's answers to provoke you. Winthrop noted various ministers' "griefe to see such opinions risen in the Country of so dangerous consequence, and so directly crossing the scope of the Gospell." However, if you were a layperson sitting on the General Court, you might be inclined to give Wheelwright the benefit of the doubt over the Mount Wollaston sermon. He insisted that he did not deny the importance of sanctification, or faith, or repentance; was this really the blatant heresy that endangered states and justified the court's interfering with the churches? Winthrop, putting a brave face on a prosecutorial retreat, wrote in his "Apology" that "this being matter of Doctrine, the Court passed it by for the present." He omitted altogether what happened next.

Deputy Spencer, Shepard's congregant, recognized that the nuances of Wheelwright's Mount Wollaston sermon were proving too confusing to demonstrate that Wheelwright was a heretic. Therefore, he turned to the basic issue that split Cotton and Wheelwright from the rest of the ministers: "*Wheelwright* teaches . . . contrary to the Doctrine preached in New-England; for . . . it is commonly taught in New-England, That a man may prove his justification by his Sanctification." The assistant John Endicott seconded Spencer: Wheelwright's doctrine, he said, "is concluded a False Doctrine, because it is a Doctrine against all the Ministers of the Country."

This line of attack also failed to produce a heresy conviction, for the simple reason that it no longer focused on Wheelwright alone; it went to the heart of Cotton's differences with his brethren. And at this critical moment, Cotton interposed himself, an intervention that Winthrop conspicuously omitted from both his journal and his "Apology": "Brother *Wheelwright's* Doctrine was according to God," Cotton announced, "in the Points Controverted, and wholely, and altogether." Go after Wheelwright, and you go after me, Cotton warned in effect. It may have been the boldest act of defiance in his entire professional career, in England or Massachusetts.

Cotton's intervention effectively closed off the prosecution's doctrinal line of pursuit—no one was prepared to argue (at least in public) that Cotton preached heresies dangerous to the state. Cotton spoke "much more" to "allay the Heat of their Raging Spirits," claimed S.G., summarizing the trial report, but it was to no avail. Spencer retreated to the issue of Wheelwright's sedition, only now stripped of its doctrinal element: "The Matter in hand is not the Doctrine, whether it be true or false: but the Question is, Whether or not Mr. *Wheelwright* hath stirred up Mutiny in the Country, and cast Aspersions upon the Ministers?" The problem with this line of attack was that Wheelwright still refused to acknowledge that he had meant the ministers—he had been making general theological statements, not attacks on specific individuals.

It was at this point that Wheelwright's prosecutors finally found their way to a conviction. Someone hit upon the clever expedient of asking the ministers if they taught the doctrines that Wheelwright condemned. The ministers, without Cotton, met overnight and the next day announced to the court that they did indeed "walk in" and teach what Wheelwright had termed a covenant of works. Cotton dissented. The other ministers, according to Winthrop, then spoke of the great dangers to church and state presented by the present religious divisions, claiming they would do everything in their power to effect a reconciliation between them and Wheelwright. They presented Wheelwright with a way to gracefully back down, charitably concluding that his being newly arrived in the colony might have been the occasion of their differences of opinion. Winthrop professed to be struck by the "humanity and respect" with which the ministers addressed Wheelwright and expressed disapproval that Wheelwright showed no willingness to reciprocate.

Collectively laying ministerial authority on the line proved effective. The ministers, save one, had said what Wheelwright refused to admit—his sermon had attacked them. When they gave Wheelwright a facesaving way to back down, he expressed no interest in reconciliation. To refuse to convict Wheelwright now would be to repudiate Massachusetts's clerical establishment for the sake of a minister who was not only theologically marginal, divisive, and largely unknown but also recklessly inflexible. Roger Williams's considerable support in Salem had dwindled when he tried to make his congregation choose between him and the rest of the churches. Similarly, while most magistrates might not have been prepared to agree with Winthrop that Wheelwright was a closet familist, they were also not prepared to agree with Wheelwright that the rest of the ministers were under a covenant of works. "The priests got two of the magistrates on their side," was how Coddington remembered the conclusion of the trial, "and so got the major part with them." How the deputies reached their own majority to convict, if it had ever been in doubt, is unknown. Wheelwright was found guilty of sedition and contempt of court (for preaching a contentious sermon on a day the Court had called for reconciliation). The heresy accusation silently vanished.

The Court deferred sentencing Wheelright until its next sitting. It was not uncommon for Massachusetts courts, like Massachusetts churches, to give sinners time to repent before determining their sentence. The delay might also have stemmed from recognition that the new majority on the Court had pushed its luck in convicting him after half its case had vanished. The Court then proceeded to other business, which included a decision to move its future sessions out of now-hostile Boston to Newtowne.

––––––

Wheelwright was now a criminal, but his conviction, rather than resolving the controversy, marked its expansion from a religious dispute into a political one. The heresy charge, which had provided the leverage to get him on trial in the first place, had vanished; what was left was the argument that sedition existed when the author of the seditious statements denied meaning what he was accused of and had the support of John Cotton. Meanwhile, the governor of the colony did not recognize that this allegedly subversive sermon was subverting his government. It was easy to interpret Wheelwright's conviction simply as persecution of a minister for preaching the truth of the gospel, easy to conclude that the result, instead of giving state legitimacy to the foes of Boston, drained the legitimacy of this infant state and gave further credibility to the claim of the most militant Bostonians that their opponents were under an antichristian covenant of works.

Wheelwright's supporters accordingly launched aggressive protests. Vane and some other members handed the Court a now-disappeared "Protestation." The Court's proceedings were null, it argued, because a minority on the Court dissented. Presumably Vane and the others reasoned that if the Court functioned as a jury in convicting Wheelwright, then its lack of unanimity voided the conviction.

Other disappointed and angry Wheelwright supporters, as they spilled into the lane outside the Boston meetinghouse, decided to register their disapproval of the Court's action. They drew up a "remonstrance and Petition." Petitioning rulers for redress of grievances was a time-honored but tricky custom in England's hierarchical, authoritarian culture. While petitioning in itself was legitimate, petitioners risked a punitive response should they imply that their rulers' conduct might be responsible for those grievances. To use an analogy, it was a commonplace observation that rulers stood in for God to those they governed, and while people routinely petitioned God with prayer about their troubles, a prayer that even hinted at rebuking God for these troubles would be a blasphemous invitation to divine retribution.

Remaining within the uncertain bounds of the acceptably deferential proved a severe challenge to the angry petitioners. Winthrop claimed that William Aspinwall, the Boston church's deacon, wrote the first draft of the petition in language so "foule" that he had to tone it down. Even toned down, however, the finished document careened dangerously in tone between deference and a belligerent defiance that no seventeenth-century English governing body would have left unpunished. Wheelwright preached the true gospel path to peace. Hence there had been no contempt of the Court's aim of bringing peace to the colony. Nor had there been sedition: Wheelwright had committed no seditious act; his doctrine could not have been seditious because it came from the Holy Ghost; and the sermon's audience had not been moved to revolt. The petition then audaciously suggested that the Court reflect if Satan were behind its action, since Satan always "raised up such calumnies against the faithfull Prophets of God." It warned the Court to "consider the danger of meddling against the Prophets of God." The petitioners closed by appealing to the Court as "nursing Fathers," which stuck the right deferential note, but added that "if wee should receive repulse from you, with the Lord wee shall find grace." The petition was not an appeal for clemency for Wheelwright; it was an offer to the Court to make amends for passing an illegitimate sentence under the influence of Satan, a sentence that invited the Lord's retribution.

That more than sixty men were prepared to sign this bellicose document, which itself would eventually be deemed seditious for its defiance of the Court, suggests the intensity of resentment stirred up by Wheelwright's conviction. Most of the petition signers were freemen, and among them were a disproportionate number of officeholders and the better-off. The great majority had been in Massachusetts for more than three years. These were respectable members of the commonwealth outraged that what they considered the gospel should be persecuted in a puritan colony.

Most of the signers came from Boston, with at least eleven from adjacent Charleston. While Winthrop at his most histrionic claimed that Anne Hutchinson was more popular than all the ministers in the colony combined, the residencies of the signers support all the other evidence indicating that "Mr. Cotton's party" was localized around Boston. Boston being the chief mercantile town in the colony, merchants and craftsmen were well represented among the protesters. Some scholars have therefore hypothesized a link between pursuing these trades and being attracted to "antinomianism," although they do not agree on what that connection was. If there was a special attraction, it was unique to Boston, since merchants and craftsmen elsewhere did not have a disproportionate attraction to antinomianism. For want of any corroborating evidence, it seems simpler to assume that previous ties from Lincolnshire and immediate proximity to Cotton and Wheelwright were far more important than professional affiliations in determining support for those ministers.

Historians use the petition to demonstrate the existence of a large contingent of "Hutchinsonians," but while it is safe to assume that any follower of Hutchinson would be a follower, in a way, of Wheelwright, there is no reason to assume the reverse. Compared with Hutchinson, Wheelwright was a theological moderate. Signing the petition might not have even indicated support of Wheelwright's theology, but rather severe reservations about an almost self-evidently problematic prosecution against a godly minister by people who had come to the New World fleeing persecution. Winthrop later said critics ranged from those who thought the Court had been unjust to those who thought it had been "(at best) over hasty." Cotton himself, although he did not sign, was furious at the Court's verdict. Having been verbally knocked around for his preaching by his opponents, he too suspected that many in Massachusetts were confusing the covenant of grace with the covenant of works. Wheelwright, therefore, had some justification in expressing himself as forcefully as he did.

It is an open question whether Wheelwright's sermon, stripped of the heresy charge and placed in the context of the other inflammatory preaching that winter, was so distinctive as to uniquely warrant a criminal charge. Sedition in this context was an emergent, political category, not a fixed legal one. There is no question, on the other hand, that the petition defending him blatantly violated accepted norms for how subjects were to address their rulers.

That violation makes all the more striking the Court's muted response to it: nothing but Winthrop's "Apology." This response was extremely mild in comparison to the severe Court reaction to the Salem letter a year and a half earlier that protested the Court's refusal to grant Salem land. As will be seen, Winthrop's restraint was not due to lack of comparable outrage at the Court's authority being challenged. Rather, it reflected hard political realities: Boston was more important than Salem; Cotton and Vane were much more influential and better connected than Williams and his supporters; and Cotton's party was still well represented in the colony's government. Wheelwright, his supporters, and Anne Hutchinson would not suffer the Salemites' fates of expulsions from the Court, jail, and banishments until these factors started to change.

———

Wheelwright's opponents very soon had the opportunity to strengthen their political hand. On May 17, the General Court met in Newtowne for the critical elections of the assistants, deputy governor, and governor. Winthrop, Dudley, Wilson, and other magistrates and ministers campaigned furiously to ensure that Vane would not be reelected. The father of the famous diarist Samuel Sewall told Samuel "many a time" how he and others traveled twenty-five miles from Newbury to Newtowne, spurred on by their minister, Thomas Parker, in order to be made freemen, vote in the election, "and help to strengthen Govr Winthrop's Party."

In the colony at large, Cotton's party had been at most tolerated, rather than actively supported. With Massachusetts's establishment campaigning against them, they could foresee in this election the demise of their already limited political power. Accordingly, they engaged in a desperate political maneuver on election day. Freemen did not need to be present but could vote by proxy. While freemen from outlying towns sent in their votes by proxy, the Boston freemen turned out in force in the field in front of the Newtowne meetinghouse for the afternoon Court meeting. The procedure on election days had been that no Court business would take place until the elections had finished, and then each town would be represented only by the freemen it had chosen as deputies, not by all the freemen who had come to vote. When the session began, however, the Bostonians asserted that the assembly was a proper meeting of the General Court, not just an election, and that the freemen were represented in person rather than by their deputies. They tried to present a petition to revoke Wheelwright's conviction, claiming it was their "liberty" to do so. Since many freemen from outlying towns were absent and voting by proxy, they were perhaps hoping that enough Boston freemen were present to overturn the conviction. They also may have thought that a direct appeal to the freemen would be more successful than one to the General Court. Governor Vane saw no problem with this unprecedented motion and wished to read the petition.

Deputy Governor Winthrop, on both principled and pragmatic grounds, disagreed and successfully struggled with his benchmate for control of the meeting. He called for the assembled freemen to decide if they wished to move to the election. The "greater number by many" did so. Vane and his allies still refused to proceed, whereupon Winthrop told him the election would take place without him. John Wilson climbed a tree and dramatically exhorted the crowd to remember their charter and the business of the day. He was answered by cries of "Election, election." Winthrop and those freemen who wanted to vote did so. Winthrop was elected governor, while Wheelwright's supporters, Vane, Coddington, and Dummer, were not reelected to any position. Vane's side uttered "fierce speeches" and resorted to physical manhandling, according to Winthrop. But they soon saw they were outnumbered and "grew quiet."

Now that the opponents of Vane and Wheelwright had firm control of the Court, they engaged in high-handed tactics of their own. The Bostonians had prepared for a colony-wide defeat by putting off their selection of deputies until they saw how the election for magistrates turned out. Thereafter, they returned home and elected Vane, Coddington, and Atherton Hough, former mayor of Boston, Lincolnshire. The General Court, being "grieved" at finding Coddington and Vane back again, annulled the election on a technicality, whereupon Boston elected them again. "The court not finding how they might reject them," in Winthrop's words, "they were admitted." According to the Court records, the initiative for rejecting the Boston deputies came from their fellow deputies, not the magistrates, which suggests how widespread disapproval of Boston was among the ordinary laity by this time. Wheelwright's defiance at his trial, the roving Boston truth squads, the belligerent Wheelwright petition, and the high-handed behavior of the Boston freemen on election day had significantly eroded tolerance for Cotton's party.

The new General Court, eleven magistrates with thirty-two deputies representing fourteen towns, quickly got down to business in the Newtowne meetinghouse. It called for a synod of the churches to determine who was correct in the colony's theological disputes. The Court then summoned Wheelwright. When he came, it told him that it was putting off sentencing him and informed him that it might show him clemency if he in turn showed repentance. Wheelwright defiantly replied that if he had really committed sedition, the Court should simply put him to death, and in any event he meant to appeal to England, "for he could retract nothing." Wheelwright was dismissed with no further consequences for his defiant words.

Wheelwright's brazen and unchallenged willingness to defy the Court reflected two serious difficulties with his conviction. First, an important portion of the population refused to accept it as just. Second, the perhaps problematic justice of the conviction invited attention to its problematic legality. The General Court had the legal authority to convict Wheelwright from its charter. The charter, however, was in the process of being revoked. Vane, son of a privy councillor, was a walking reminder that there were higher and more important sources of legal authority than that possessed by the people who convicted Wheelwright. With Vane behind him, Wheelwright felt free to defy the Court, and the Court hesitated to act against him. Wheelwright's threat of an appeal to the king was probably only the tip of an iceberg of discussions about the authority of King Charles and of Vane's access to Charles's court. It may have been at this point that Vane's supporters started talking about Charles appointing him governor-general of Massachusetts. Vane, busy undermining the authority of the General Court, certainly did not discourage this sort of talk.

While Vane's connections bolstered his supporters, they caused his opponents to weave extraordinary, fearful fantasies about the menace he presented. Just how extraordinary those fantasies could get is shown by a letter that Shepard wrote to Winthrop a few days after the election. The letter critiqued a now-lost response by Winthrop to a "Remonstrance" written by Vane and other members of the Court (probably the same document as their "Protestation" mentioned above). Winthrop had not put enough twigs on his lash against the remonstrants, Shepard complained. He had treated Vane with a courtesy Vane did not deserve. Vane was "the prime craftsman of forging all our late novelties, the Sheba of our distractions." His principles had "sown the seed of confusion of this and all states in the world," and "it may be," Shepard fretted, "he is now hatching evill agaynst this place."

With the well-connected Vane hatching evils against Massachusetts, the wide and empty expanses of the Atlantic Ocean began to hint at awful terrors, akin to the nightmares about Catholic invasions that periodically swept regions of England. Winthrop repeated rumors that "many" Grindletonians (a familist-inspired sect) were about to arrive to reinforce the ranks of the "erronists." The chronicler Edward Johnson reported that the election petition had been intended to delay the elections because the radicals' numbers were swelling so quickly that delay would enable them to gain control of the Court. It would have required many boatloads of heretics to reach that point. When the General Court in November finally identified males that it perceived as seriously dissident, its total came to perhaps one in twenty-five in the colony as a whole.

This combination of the Vane-Wheelwright faction's contempt for the General Court's authority and the Court's culturally normative paranoia in the face of determined dissent drove Shepard to make an open political intervention. Preaching to the Court, he warned it that Massachusetts stood on the brink of bloody anarchy. Wheelwright's threat to appeal to the king was an effort to break down the "the walls of Magistracy." The Bostonians' behavior on election day stemmed from "confusion, the mother of discord among the people." The current abuse of the ministers, Shepard insisted, would result in their all being "massacred."

Shepard expressed not only alarm at the present situation but indignation at those who refused to accept the magnitude of the crisis. Toleration of the Bostonians "for peace sake" would "ruin the Gospel" and end up with "Gods Ordinances in the purity of them removed." He had been arguing with skeptics who maintained that enemies "will not assault us first by craft and subtilty, but openly and violently." That attitude would result in "oppressors set over you, to remove ordinances, to encrease your burdens." Shepard closed his address with a dramatic rhetorical question: "Would you have this state in time to degenerate into Tyranny? . . . Be gentle and open the door to all comers that may cut our throats in time."

Shepard's harangue against opening the door to an invasion of heretics fell on receptive and perhaps prepared ears. The Court passed a law forbidding any town or individual to take in strangers for more than three weeks whom the magistrates had not permitted to stay, or face crippling fines. When the Grindletonians made their landing, they could be legally repulsed.

Yet it is hard to read Shepard's harsh, violent polemic and his letter to Winthrop and not conclude that he wanted a good deal more than that — stiffer and immediate action against Wheelwright and Greensmith, a firmer crackdown on deviant opinions, probably some kind of action against Vane, and more of an effort on Winthrop's part to convince people that enemies of the state would move by craft and subtlety before they moved openly. The gap between what Shepard wanted and what the Court actually produced suggests Winthrop's restraining role among those in pursuit of Wheelwright and Vane.

That suggestion is no accident. We know, for example, next to nothing about the machinations of Winthrop's deputy governor, the ex-soldier Thomas Dudley, who in general was a harsher man than Winthrop and disapproved of Winthrop's leniency. Both before and after the present disturbances, Dudley and Winthrop clashed over the amount of patience to be shown to religious dissenters. "Hate heresie — make blessed ends" were Dudley's final words of advice to his family.

Dudley had moved from Newtowne to remote Ipswich after Hooker left in 1636, but in 1637, due to the "necessity of the Government and importunity of friends," he moved to Roxbury, adjacent to Boston. His role in this dispute was widely praised. Hubbard recalled Dudley as "the most resolved champion of the truth, above all the gentlemen in the country." An anonymous memorial verse gives him much the same credit. According to a manuscript account of his life, it was due to "Mr Dudleys courage and constancy to the truth [that] things issued well." Thus, it was Dudley, not Winthrop, who was the most important magisterial hard-liner against Vane and his allies, although his machinations have left almost no traces. If we had a fuller account of the politics of the controversy, Winthrop even more clearly would appear a moderate among the activists against Cotton's party, restraining the Court's most aggressive members and frustrating the most aggressive ministers, among whom Shepard was surely not alone.

Shepard's harangue to the Court was, in all likelihood, part of one side of a debate. Winthrop presented the other, winning side when he explained in his journal why the Court did not move immediately against Wheelwright and what Winthrop called his "insolent" supporters: "The intent of the court in deferring the sentence was, that . . . having now power enough to have crushed them, their moderation and desire of reconciliation might appear to all."

Winthrop's restraint in the spring of 1637 was based on a genuine, if limited, desire of reconciliation, as he claimed. It was almost certainly also based on a more realistic assessment than Shepard and Dudley's of the General Court's effective power against people of the stature of Vane and Cotton. He wrote in his journal that his side now had the power to "crush" their opponents. Vane and his allies had no inhibitions about showing that they were not impressed. Winthrop, gentry-by-the-fingernails, had wrested the governorship back from Vane, who was by breeding and connections as aristocratic as one could get without being titled. No matter how many elections Winthrop and his side won in their tiny colony of about eight thousand people, in an English context they remained relatively low on the scale of status and power. Should Winthrop forget that he was "but an attorney," Vane's supporters were all too happy to remind him.

Winthrop carefully noted the various snubs his fellow church members gave him after he was elected governor. Halberds provided the opportunity for perhaps the most notorious of the petty incidents. Four militia sergeants from Boston bearing these combination spears and battle-axes marched as an honor guard before Vane to the May

General Court, just as they marched before him whenever he went to any public event, including church services. When Winthrop wrested the governorship back on election day, the Boston sergeants laid down their halberds and went home. There were no sergeants waiting to attend him when he returned to Boston. The sergeants later explained to Winthrop that they had served Vane not because he was governor but because of his eminence. Winthrop felt the affront to his honor keenly. He argued back that, regardless of Vane's superior social rank, they had to do the same for him, "because the place drowns the person, be he honorable or base." Moreover, having once bestowed the honor on Vane in office, they could not take it away "without contempt or injury." Cotton urged moderation on Boston, and other towns offered to send halberd bearers. Boston thereupon offered to provide men, but the sergeants themselves still refused. Winthrop elected to use two of his own servants, "whereas," as he brooded in his journal, "the former governor never had less than four."

The most serious of the snubs the Bostonians delivered Winthrop and his government came in connection with the war against the Pequot Indians of Connecticut. In April, with Vane as governor, the General Court assigned each town a quota of men for a campaign against them. The expedition climaxed in the massacre of six to seven hundred Pequot men, women, and children on May 24. This "divine slaughter," as Shepard later called it, made the English participants, or the less squeamish of them, feel that they were back in the glorious days of the Old Testament, mowing down their heathen enemies. In June the General Court organized another expedition. But now, claimed Winthrop, Boston provided only a couple of church members "whom they cared not to be rid of" and a few others "of the most refuse sort." Wilson had been the minister chosen by lot to accompany the expedition, and no one from Boston even bade him farewell.

According to Winthrop, Boston's action was intended as a protest against the recent government turnover: "The former Governour and some of the Magistrates then were friends of Christ and Free-grace, but the present were enemies, &c. Antichrists, persecutors." One Bostonian agreed with Winthrop's explanation and accounted for this and the incident of the halberds in highly personal terms. "Inequality of observance" came from "the affection which some designed to those offices, bore to the then Governor Sr. *He: Vane,* who by his noble, affable and discreet carriage, ingaged their utmost attention." Both Winthrop and the present government of Massachusetts, according to the Bostonian, were characterized by "despicableness." It is vivid testimony of how invisible Vane's importance is to scholars that while they routinely repeat this anecdote, they emphasize the snub to Wilson and ignore entirely that the Boston protest was intended mainly as an affirmation of Vane.

These increasingly aggressive gestures toward Winthrop and the General Court's authority were accompanied by an increasingly intolerant atmosphere in the Boston church. The earlier ecumenical church, which could contain in peaceful coexistence ministers and laypeople as various as Wilson and Cotton, Winthrop and Hutchinson, had broken down. Winthrop bitterly claimed that now none could be admitted to the church who did not renounce their sanctification and "waite for an immediate revelation of the Spirit." Those already in the church (like Winthrop) who would not "do the same, and acknowledge this new light, and say as they say," would be "presently noted, and under-esteemed." Young Giles Firmin, who returned to Boston in June or July after a four-year absence, described much the same kind of pressure to conform: "Divers have lain looking for, and listening after such a word [from the Bible], set home by an impulse of the Spirit, and all other wayes of evidencing [salvation] are neglected." Finding assurance by the evidence of holiness, said Firmin, was "cryed down, as being no sure or sound way of evidencing: Hence, many poor, but sincere Christians, were afraid and dare not go this way to work."

We can only wonder how many members of the Boston congregation genuinely found comfort through what they thought was the witness of the Spirit, and how many accepted it simply because of their admiration for those persons insisting on it. Conversely, we can also only wonder how many were, as Firmin suggests, trapped in a no-man's-land, not daring to search themselves for signs that they had been saved, as that would put them under a covenant of works, while being unable to experience the Spirit's comfort. A Boston woman in spiritual despair that summer, for example, threw her infant in a well to settle in her own mind that she was damned. Perhaps she would not have come to such a crisis in another congregation. Firmin may have felt this narrowing of options for assurance as particularly threatening, since he wrestled with severe doubts about his salvation for all of a very long life. Another recently arrived immigrant, after listening to the Bostonians' arguments, decided, as had others, that they were motivated by "envy" of the ministers. She chose to go to Salem, which was "more free." What to a preacher like Wheelwright and perhaps to many of the Boston laity had been an effort to liberate Christians from "servile fear" resulted for Firmin and Winthrop in a narrow, intolerant, superficial, and self-deluded community whose concept of assurance dangerously bypassed most of the transformative work required in the genuine process of conversion and was more inaccessible to sincere, struggling Christians than to hypocrites.

Presumably Hutchinson was at the height of her local prestige, as events seemed to confirm her earlier critique of Massachusetts's ministers. She must have played a large role in the growing intolerance, warning women at childbirths with increasing stridency to beware the ministers' preaching and dropping hints that there was more to be learned of the gospel's truths than even Cotton had revealed. Perhaps her and her female allies' departures every Sunday when Wilson rose to preach had become almost routinized.

The meetings at Hutchinson's house must have reached their peak of popularity. Sixty or eighty attended her twice-weekly "lectures," according to Winthrop, who could have counted from his window. Boston's population in 1637 may have been around a thousand, which means that at the peak of the controversy roughly a quarter of the town's adults visited Hutchinson's home on any given week. There would have been a variety of reasons bringing people to her house: news, debate, curiosity, solidarity, spiritual growth, sharing of grievances, and a chance to talk in a group without Wilson or Winthrop present.

Winthrop and his allies considered the meetings in Hutchinson's house the focal point for theological and political dissidence in the colony. From their perspective, they were probably correct, but we know very little about what took place at them. The meetings at their peak were of two kinds, one for men and women, and one for women only. Hutchinson led the women's meeting; we do not know who led the mixed one. She went over Cotton's sermons in a highly selective manner and answered questions raised by the sermons, putting her own spin on them. Cotton claimed that when he sent "Sisters of the Church" to report on her meetings, "no speech fell from her, that could be much excepted against." It is probable that had it been Shepard and not Cotton sending "sisters," there might have been a great deal that would have been "much excepted against."

We have only a couple of insider descriptions of Hutchinson's meetings. She was said to lead them sitting "gravely" on a chair (chairs were rare items in the colony, and a mark of distinction). A sympathetic Boston insider noted that she liked having followers. He described how Jane Hawkins, a Boston midwife, ex-puritan trance prophetess, and rumored witch, played on this desire by being the first to agree with Hutchinson whenever she advanced some new doctrinal notion. As a result, she frequently got fed in the Hutchinson household. Hawkins "followed Christ for *loaves*" was the jaundiced contemporary remark.

As that anecdote suggests, even allies of Hutchinson did not view her uncritically. Giles Firmin related how he heard Hutchinson in the summer of 1637 assert at her own dinner table that Cotton had said there was no difference between the graces of saints and hypocrites. Members of her household told her that he had said no such thing. Boston may have been increasingly radicalized, but it was no "Hutchinsonian" monolith.

CHAPTER 6

The Churches on Fire

Summer 1637

As a result of the spring's political strife, Cotton's party was an isolated minority in the fragile colony. Its opponents, however, in spite of Winthrop's brave talk, lacked the means to "crush" them. This was not a situation with long-term viability for either side. "The churches are on fire!" fishermen shouted to the immigrant ships sailing into Boston harbor. Something was going to have to give in this struggle, and what that something was and how it gave would determine if Anne Hutchinson was tried.

─────

As Cotton's party increasingly distanced itself from the churches and government of Massachusetts, the Court order against immigrants awaited its first test. On July 12 a ship with Lincolnshire immigrants, including Anne's brother-in-law Samuel Hutchinson, arrived. The magistrates grilled the newcomers on whether they knew Wheelwright and demanded that they disavow his doctrine. When the immigrants would not do so, the magistrates gave them four months to remain in the colony. The magistrates' treatment of the immigrants might have been defensible had the General Court condemned Wheelwright's teachings at his trial. But it had not, and Winthrop stressed that Wheelwright's conviction was not based on his doctrine.

Cotton's party was understandably furious. The magistrates had no problem in admitting blasphemers and profane persons to Massachusetts, their angry talk went, but they drew the line at true Christians. Moreover, the Bostonians worried, accurately enough, if the General Court felt free to keep out immigrants because they agreed with Wheelwright, how long would it be before it felt free to banish his supporters who were already in the colony?

While the opponents of Boston saw Vane and his allies as engaged in a conspiracy to secretly undermine the colony, Boston saw its liberty, both Christian and secular, being trodden down by an illegitimate government. It is not surprising that for many in Cotton's party, the order against the immigrants, mild though it was, was the last straw. Vane wrote a protest in which he warned that the order was an infringement on the liberties of Englishmen and the king's rights, and that the colony need not be surprised if Charles took steps to defend those rights. Given Vane's connections at Charles's court and the fact the Massachusetts charter had been legally revoked on May 3, this was no idle threat. Since it is common to portray the conflict in Massachusetts as a struggle of individual conscience against the state, it should be noted that Vane agreed heartily that the colony had the right to keep out people who had incorrect beliefs — but these newcomers did not fall in that category.

Angry Bostonians did more than complain. Winthrop recorded in his journal that in response to the Court's order, the "other party" was starting to talk about leaving the colony. Characteristically, he did not record that one of those people was Cotton.

As Cotton later acknowledged, he, along with many in his church, was furious about Wheelwright's conviction and Samuel Hutchinson's denied residency. When godly people like these were being persecuted, clearly the disciplinary apparatus of the state had gone askew. Moreover, although members of the Boston church like Winthrop had played a role in this persecution, Boston's disciplinary mechanisms were themselves blocked, for the General Court would protect Winthrop. Nor could outside churches be called in to settle the dispute, because they, too, had prominent members hostile to Cotton's party.

The checks and balances of Cotton's godly commonwealth had failed. Prevented from applying the church sanctions that the situation called for, Cotton later recalled that he "verily purposed openly to have protested against all such proceedings as I took to be injurious and offensive and to have departed into some other parts of this Country." His intention was reinforced by a petition with about sixty signatures (almost certainly all male) expressing a willingness to move with him. The Hutchinson family would have been well represented among the signers. Although the sources get somewhat murky at this point, Vane and Cotton seem to have employed Roger Williams to buy land for them from the Narragansett Indians.

Now might have been the time when Anne Hutchinson and the other radicals thought themselves on the verge of triumph. The great Cotton and Wheelwright, along with their supporters, would finally separate themselves from the influence of Massachusetts's antichristian leaders. Surely, in a new colony they would become more open to the deeper gospel truths the radicals had to offer them. This new colony, permeated with true gospel principles, would become the vanguard of the struggle against Antichrist and for bringing in the millennium.

Now was also the moment when Massachusetts's survival was perhaps most in question. The efforts of the opponents of Cotton and his allies to resolve a heated religious dispute through political means had brought the colony to the verge of self-destruction. Wheelwright was expendable; Anne Hutchinson would not be greatly missed; but the departure of Cotton and his prominent supporters would have shattered the morale of the colony and wrecked its standing among English puritans. Having the son of a privy councillor setting up a rival, hostile colony at a time when Massachusetts's charter was officially dead would make the colony's precarious standing no easier with the English government.

But Cotton did not leave. For reasons now lost, the effort to purchase land that summer failed. Anne Hutchinson would remain in the colony until the following spring, and when she, along with many others, finally left, she would be joined by neither Cotton nor Vane. Over the next three-quarters of a year, Cotton's party, not Massachusetts, would break up, and Hutchinson's trials would be among the consequences.

———

Perhaps because of the land purchase failure, Vane departed for England on August 3, 1637. Vane promised his supporters he would return, and he almost certainly talked of returning as governor-general — news of the revocation of the charter could easily have reached Massachusetts by this time. Winthrop recorded that "Mr. Vane's party" gathered to see him off at the harbor, firing guns and cannon in his honor.

To Vane's opponents, still reeling from four months of political struggle, he was not someone to be honored. A letter to England summarized his rule by saying that he promoted Boston doctrines "with such violence, as if they had been matters of that consequence that the peace and welfare of New-England must be sacrificed, rather than they should not take place. . . . He hath kindled those sparks among us, which many ages will not be able to undo." Vane's "misguidings and bad conduct," lamented William Hubbard, "much eclipsed" Massachusetts's "beauty, place, and splendor." Once Vane was gone, Winthrop wrote a reply to his attack on the immigration law. Winthrop's response denounced Vane as a religious fanatic with an embittered mind, who by his appeals to the authority of the king was undermining the entire colony to protect his party.

Thomas Shepard was even harsher in his appraisal, unsurprisingly, when he preached the election-day sermon in May 1638. Shepard devoted the sermon to Vane, thinly disguised as Abimelech, the "young courtier," the bloody son of the good and pious Old Testament ruler Gideon, who upon Gideon's death made himself king. Shepard gave a close analysis of how Abimelech rose to power, and the remarkable way recent Massachusetts history mirrored scripture was not likely to be lost on any of his audience.

Abimelech, the "bramble," climbed to power by making a faction for himself. He knew that in a religious country, "people will be made into a faction but by shows of religion." He therefore adopted the same cunning plan as the Catholic Spanish had done in Holland (at least according to paranoid Protestants like Shepard): create a zealous party ostensibly promoting true religion, like the Dutch Protestant Arminians, and use it as a front to take over the country. Abimelech therefore "advanceth another religion than what they had under Gideon . . . a god of a new covenant." Having spread the new religion, he would "scratch and rent and disfigure all magistrates and ministers . . . fight against them, kill them [he would cry], they are worse then Pilate and Scribes and Pharisees." Abimelech's crowning action in forming his faction, said Shepard, was to sow the "seeds of undermining principles of government." To that end, Abimelech asked, as Vane and his "faction" had done after Wheelwright's conviction, "Is it not fit to make appeales [just as Wheelwright had threatened to appeal to the king]? Is not the sentence of a major part of court without consent of minor a nullity [just as Vane had claimed that

Wheelwright's conviction was void because a minority on the General Court disagreed]?"

While Abimelech assembled his faction, "you will see him so humble and for publicke good." But he "intends publicke ruin." His goal was to "take away magistrate and minister . . . and then looke for fire." Vane's faction had laid siege to the religion, laws, and government of Massachusetts as dupes to advance Vane's power, and by only a hairbreadth had Massachusetts escaped bloody tyranny.

Public ruin, fire, faction, another religion — add to the dire list Shepard's earlier intimations about Jesuit conspiracies and fears about the ministers being massacred, along with the original suspicions that Vane was a spy from Charles's court to betray Massachusetts. The sum suggests the wildest suspicions that drove the opposition to Vane in the spring of 1637. Vane was an agent of Catholicism aiming at the defeat of the Reformation, like Archbishop Laud and Charles's other evil councillors. The leap of logic involved in inferring a Catholic plot from Protestant radicalism might seem vast, but it was not so daunting to seventeenth-century minds given to analyzing events in dualistic, conspiratorial terms. Puritans on both sides of the Atlantic frequently imagined Jesuit plotting behind the activities of more radical puritans. Vane thought it worth his while in his death speech before he was beheaded for treason by Charles II in 1662 to deny that he had anything to do with "Jesuitism or Popery."

Shepard's analysis of Vane was not that much different from that of Winthrop, who saw Vane as secretly undermining the colony in order to shelter his party. Neither analysis invited compromise. Winthrop, however, was a far wiser politician than Shepard, who called for "hatchets" when dealing with a bramble like Abimelech. But when Vane's ship pulled out of Boston harbor, signaling an end to the worst domestic political crisis Massachusetts's government faced until the American Revolution, Winthrop had the fort on Castle Island fire five volleys in his honor (although perhaps fired as well in joy at his departure). The focal point for resistance to the General Court and to the theological consensus of most of the colony's ministers, "the great Favourer and Maintainer of these Errors" and the man who "did animate that Faction," as Boston church member Giles Firmin called him, was gone, if only perhaps for the time being. In what might have been its own way of celebrating the shifting balance of power in Massachusetts, the General Court finally threw Bostonian Stephen Greensmith in prison for his continued refusal to pay his fine for insulting the ministers, and it ignored his threat to appeal his sentence to the king.

———

As Vane left, his opponents made a determined effort to pull Cotton to their side and keep him in the colony. To that end Governor Winthrop and Deputy Governor Dudley met with Cotton. Winthrop and Dudley assured him that they could live with his theology, and they purred soothing explanations into his ear about the rough treatment of his allies that had so enraged him. Wheelwright, they told him, had been punished not for heresy but for sedition. Samuel Hutchinson and other Lincolnshire immigrants were denied residency in Massachusetts because, like the theological radicals and unlike Cotton and Wheelwright, they denied that converts' human nature had any holiness. Cotton, in a major shift, persuaded himself to accept those claims, which must have required some hard swallowing. The magistrates had asserted all along that Wheelwright had not been punished for his opinions. For some of the magistrates at least, that claim was patently not true, and up until now, it had not stopped Cotton from regarding Wheelwright's conviction as unjustified. Wheelwright reminded Cotton later that Samuel Hutchinson believed nothing more radical than Wheelwright. Hutchinson was in Boston for Cotton to talk to, and he may have been accepted as a member of the church.

In another bit of backtracking, Cotton also finally accepted Wilson's long-standing explanation that Wilson's speech of the previous December in the General Court had not been directed at Cotton or Wheelwright. Cotton announced his new conclusion to his congregation — "This sudden change was much observed by some," Winthrop drily noted. It would not be Cotton's last sudden change.

Cotton had a number of reasons to persuade himself that his reasons for leaving Massachusetts were mistaken. With Vane gone, he had lost the last of his magisterial supporters. Events might be pushing him to a split with his brethren and to the literal role of prophet in the wilderness, but playing that kind of dissident, a role in which Roger Williams thrived, had never been Cotton's forte. Through charm, bribes, and evasion, he had made his peace with bishops as long as they were willing to make peace with him. Surely he should be able to make his peace with the puritans of Massachusetts. The failure of the land purchase in Narragansett Bay meant that there would be no move that year anyway. Perhaps, too, when faced with the serious prospect of departing, Cotton discovered the depths of his commitment to the church order he had played a large role in shaping.

But what brought the magistrates to the table? Winthrop, unlike some of his allies, all along had distinguished between Cotton and the more radical members of his congregation, even to the point of willfully toning down his descriptions of Cotton's behavior and attitudes. Dudley, however, is another matter. It is unfortunate that such an important person shows up rarely in the surviving documents. When he does make an appearance, his attitude toward Cotton is strikingly different from Winthrop's: sarcastic, hostile, and impatient. Dudley seems to have looked upon Cotton with as much suspicion as Shepard did. In Dudley's congregation at Roxbury, defending Cotton's theology too vigorously could get a member excommunicated. And yet Dudley was prepared to say to Cotton's face that he could live with his doctrine.

Perhaps Winthrop pointed out some hard truths to Dudley. The colony had lost Thomas Hooker the year before, which already raised eyebrows in England. The newly arrived famous minister John Davenport and his wealthy Londoner followers were making noises about finding another colony. Key English puritan magnates were encouraging Connecticut's development. Massachusetts was already close to the brink because of the revocation of its charter and the broadcasting in England of its squabbles. The immigrants streaming into the port of Boston could always move on to Connecticut, and the last thing Winthrop wanted to have to do was explain to them why the town was half empty or more and the most famous minister in the colony gone. Not only would Cotton's departure be a blow to the colony's credibility; he would take with him some of its wealthiest and most important merchants. I picture Dudley, who thought that Cotton's doctrine was at best illogical, fuming, swallowing his well-developed heresy-hunting instincts, then painfully telling Cotton that his teaching was acceptable — and thereafter, as various trial accounts show, striking out at him whenever circumstances allowed.

On August 5, the ministers Thomas Hooker and John Wilson came in a group from Connecticut. The party brought news of the end of Pequot resistance and Indian slaves to distribute. With the arrival of the ministers, preparations for the synod commenced. Synods were the vital third leg in the Massachusetts stool of discipline. Secular courts and the churches enforced the word of God; synods authoritatively determined what the word of God meant. The upcoming synod would succeed only if the ministers could reach some sort of agreement on that meaning. Of necessity, an agreement would require that Cotton openly repudiate the speculation of Anne Hutchinson and the other radicals. Massachusetts's survival hinged on the further breaking up of Cotton's party.

Cotton and the other ministers held extensive conferences before the synod, and in them Cotton made his first major split with Wheelwright. He reached his conclusion (probably at this time; the evidence is circumstantial) that the theological differences between him and the extreme preparationists were, as he put it in a conciliatory statement, "logicall, not theologicall." The conclusion that Hooker and Shepard were not crypto-Catholics made it easier for him to make peace with them. Wheelwright, however, would never concede this point. Meanwhile, Cotton and the other ministers agreed to narrow the differences between them to five specific points that had been fundamental to their quarrel. These points were to be debated at the synod.

The ministers also busied themselves collecting radical opinions circulating among the Boston laity. These eighty-two "errors" (as they were called from the start) they planned to refute at the synod, hopefully with Cotton's assent. Hutchinson was said by a Boston insider to have held most of them; a few appear elsewhere only in a book that Vane published in 1654.

Otherwise attaching specific opinions to specific individuals is sheer guesswork. We know of the religious development at this time of only one, probably singular radical in any detail, Boston's Captain John Underhill. Underhill, a professional soldier and a "lusty big man," for a long time was uncertain about the colony's theological disputes. However, a related set of concerns and events tipped the scale for him. He wanted badly to sleep with the wife of the cooper Joseph Febar. During the Pequot campaign, he had a revelation that his own wife and the cooper would die and that he would then marry the cooper's

wife. Underhill asserted, while smoking a pipe the Holy Spirit revealed an absolute promise of free grace to him "with such assurance
and joy, as he never since doubted of his good estate, neither should
he, though he should fall into sin." After six months of persuasion, the
cooper's wife made love with him and, he claimed, came totally under
his will. He could enjoy her three or four times a day, he boasted to a
fellow ship passenger, Jane Holmes, while returning to Massachusetts
in 1638. When trying to seduce Holmes, he told her that Febar's wife
had told him that she could be driven off from her self-deluded
confidence in her own righteousness only "by a gross act." Holmes
rebuked him, but he replied that "he knew how it was between him
and God." Underhill told Holmes that he "held nothing but what Mr.
Cotton held." He may have eventually argued that he committed
adultery to exalt free grace.

Underhill's adultery did not become public, or at least general,
knowledge until September 1638, but it is easy to imagine that he
shared his theological opinions before then, and that they might have
ended up at the synod in the most extreme "errors" about immediate
revelations, the unavoidability of sin, or the unimportance of attending
church. Underhill embodied Shepard's worst nightmares about Boston
doctrines, and he probably made the serious biblical exegetes in the
community uncomfortable and defensive. As one Bostonian asked,
"Shall every little errour touching *Divinity* in militarie men, whose
stirred humours may easily attenuate the spirits, when they so apply
themselves, and refine them into a *nicety*, be heighten'd into heresie?"

The synod opened on August 30 at the Newtowne meetinghouse with
about twenty-five ministers in attendance. In addition, the New England churches sent an unknown number of ruling lay elders, along
with "messengers" or representatives of the ordinary laity. Connecticut and Massachusetts magistrates also attended. It seems safe to
imagine well over a hundred men as participants, with an unknown
number of men and women as spectators. In the jammed, plain building, those attending might have felt awe at the sight of so many saints
and illustrious ministers gathered together, free to practice the pure
discipline of the New Testament while England sank deeper into an
Antichristian darkness. They would have prayed earnestly that God

deliver them from Satan's fogs of error and confusion, and they would have felt grim anger at the instruments of Satan who had made this synod necessary (with widely different lists of who those instruments might be). A few persons might have found their thoughts straying to the sizable bill that the colony would have to foot for food and lodging for all the delegates.

Almost immediately, the synod demonstrated its effectiveness as a tool for breaking up Cotton's party. The delegates spent the first week debating, or, rather, preparing to condemn, the errors. Although surely no one seriously thought that the synod would approve opinions labeled "errors" from the start, anyone was invited to defend them. No one was to be accused of the opinion they defended, unless they declared themselves in favor of it, an offer that meant very little in practice.

Two messengers from the Boston church, William Aspinwall and John Coggeshall, took the synod's invitation to defend errors at face value, to Cotton's surprise and alarm. He told them that their defense would make the whole Boston church guilty by association. Aspinwall and Coggeshall replied that they did not necessarily agree with those opinions, yet considering "the tendernesse of some Consciences," they could not condemn them. Cotton later claimed that Coggeshall was, with Hutchinson, one of the two ringleaders of the theological radicals.

According to Cotton, this was the first time he realized that there was a "real and broad difference" between himself and the most radical members of his congregation. That claim must be taken with a grain of salt. The errors Coggeshall and Aspinwall wanted to defend had been debated in the Boston meetinghouse, and Cotton had preached against them. Presumably Cotton had previously chosen to take seriously the claim that these were only inquiries among persons who were basically sound, which is how they were probably presented — "misexpressions," as he later put it. He had certainly assumed that such persons would have better sense than try to defend them in an environment less sympathetic than the Boston church. Cotton claimed that after his firm rebuke the messengers left the synod, and their absence "did much what forbear any prosecution of arguments in such causes." Winthrop claimed they left because he warned them that he would arrest them if they continued on with a string of procedural objections they were making. On September 3, four days after the synod's start, Anne Hutchinson's brother-in-law Edward Hutchinson had his son baptized in the Boston meetinghouse with the name of Ichabod. Presumably everyone gathered for the event knew the translation from the Hebrew: the glory has departed. The next day, the synod condemned the list of errors, with Cotton giving a qualified assent.

With lay errors out of the way, the synod moved on to its most critical topic, the nine theological points in dispute between Cotton and Wheelwright and the other ministers. After some written exchanges, the ministers commenced open debate. The tension and mutual suspicion must have been extremely high. At one point, Wheelwright made (or was pushed into) some very rash statements. They were so evocative of antinomianism and familism that Cotton later called his expressions "unsafe," and Wheelwright himself later termed them "unsafe and obscure." This is the only surviving criticism from either Cotton or Wheelwright of Wheelwright's doctrines, which gives some idea of how horrified those statements must have made other ministers.

Perhaps in angry response to equally rash statements on the other side, Cotton blindsided the proceedings with an extraordinary request. Most ministers argued that a believer's God-given faith was active at the moment of justification. Cotton insisted that it was passive and that a faith that was passive could not be observed for assurance of salvation. Now he asked for debate on the more extreme thesis that God justified sinners before they had faith at all. His thesis might have eliminated human involvement in salvation entirely and supported numerous antinomian and familist possibilities. If Cotton held to it, the synod would have collapsed in failure.

An entire day was spent in debate on Cotton's new proposition. According to Cotton's grandson, Cotton Mather, who was working from a detailed manuscript account, this debate was the most intense of the proceedings, with "much sorrowful discourse" and "solemn speeches . . . made with tears." Radicals in the audience must have been delighted to see Cotton finally in combat, while perhaps now was the time when the ministers most suspicious of him were most vocal. The minister John Norton, remembering years later, was impressed with Cotton's "singular patience" and said he was "a Mirror for the temperament, mildness, and government of his spirit" — one wonders what the provocations were that allowed him to display these virtues so conspicuously.

The discourse, sorrowful though it might have been, was not unproductive. It led to Cotton having a slight but critical change of mind. He concluded not only that justification took place with the presence of faith but that faith was more than passive in the process, as his opponents insisted. As they also insisted, a more than passive faith was implicitly a faith that could be observed for assurance of salvation, and therefore they were not promulgating a damnable covenant of works. Perhaps Anne Hutchinson was a shocked spectator the next morning when Cotton stood up in the assembly and announced his consent with them on this point. He gave "an excellent speech tending to accommodation," according to Cotton Mather.

With Cotton's concession that introspection, as well as revelations, might give assurance of salvation, he abandoned the central rallying point that tied together all the wings of his coalition. His allies understandably felt deserted — the "sectaries," Mather noted, "tried by all the obstreperous ways imaginable to hinder the reconciliation." Three years later, Cotton wrote to a still-angry Wheelwright, "May not the sight of Faith be some cause of the sight of Justification without straine of Heresy?"

The dismay of Cotton's supporters at seeing him abandon them on this critical point probably only heightened the appreciation of the other ministers. All the ministers except Wheelwright quickly worked out a final compromise statement. The statement embodied Cotton's concession about faith, insisting that sanctification must always be coexistent and at least possibly co-apparent with Cotton's witness of the Spirit, or else that witness must be considered either a "delusion or doubtful." While at first glance it would appear that all the movement was from Cotton's side, arm-twisting had to take place in both directions. The final statement about the witness of the Spirit and sanctification was a masterpiece of equivocation. It could be interpreted as supporting the majority ministerial position. On close reading, however, it could also be taken as meaning that sanctification, although "possibly" visible, in practice never reliably was until God had sent you an absolute promise of salvation. This position was not too far from where Cotton had started out. Nonetheless, he had built bridges to his fellow ministers, and, no less important, it would now be impossible for radicals like Hutchinson to claim that they were only elaborating what Cotton taught.

Just as Cotton cut the ground out from under his allies by what he was no longer willing to defend, he cut the ground out from under them by what he was no longer willing to attack. He signaled clearly that the doctrinal enemies who had argued that sanctification could be a first evidence of salvation or, even worse, who argued like Hooker that preparation for salvation was in itself saving, were not enemies anymore. Although those ministers' doctrines had not changed; although they undercut Wheelwright's Boston appointment and undertook a covert effort to get him convicted; although they savaged Boston doctrine and individuals from the pulpit; and although they pushed to get supporters of Wheelwright excluded from the colony, Cotton's distance from them was no longer equivalent to the gulf between heaven and hell. Wheelwright was left on his own. The "sectaries" were understandably upset.

Before breaking up on September 22, the synod made some other nonbinding resolutions chiefly concerned with restoring ecclesiastical order and respect for ministers. It found no biblical basis for sixty or more people to meet every week to listen to a woman in a private house answer theological questions. That last resolution is sometimes taken as a general assault on women's liberty. But if it did give out any general message, it was that should any layperson organize large meetings in which problematic doctrines were advanced and the ministers attacked, they could assume that the authorities would get upset.

———

As a piece of theater, the Synod of 1637 was impressive. The ministers, with their combination of university learning and piety, decisively identified and unanimously rejected the ignorant path of scriptural error, represented by people like Hutchinson. The Bible had one meaning; the ministers with their expertise agreed on what that meaning was; therefore the foundations of Massachusetts's godly biblical commonwealth were secure. Nine months earlier the ministers had beseeched Cotton that they "all may think and speak and preach the very same thing." Otherwise, they warned him, the laity "will be not a little disheartened and unsettled." Now the ministers were more or less in accord, and the relief of much of the laity was palpable. Edward

Johnson was impressed by the sight of so many "ministers of Christ (who were so experienced in the Scripture, that some of them could tell you the place, both Chapter and Verse, of most sentences of Scripture could be named unto them)." He waxed eloquent over them, "with scriptures light, clearing up the truths of Christ clouded by any of these Errors and Heresies." Johnson rejoiced that Christ caused "his servants in this Synod, mutually to agree" and thereby broke in pieces the "contrived plot" to draw away Cotton. Weld claimed that the Synod "strengthened" over the "indifferent" and "settled" the "wavering." The Scituate church was surely not expressing isolated sentiments when it held a day of thanksgiving for the "Reconcilliation betwixt Mr Cotton and the other ministers."

But the success of the synod should not be exaggerated. Wheelwright presumably went down fighting all the way, syllogizing, making fine scholastic distinctions, using Greek and Latin terms, and citing Reformed authorities — there was no reason for his supporters to think that the learning of the universities had condemned his reading of scripture. Moreover, the ministerial united front, such as it was, was attained after some very tense debate and only by an extremely ambiguous final statement. Even that statement to a large degree represented a papering over of differences, not a resolution of them. The ministers in effect simply stated that they were all among the godly, whatever their differences, and that, to quote a contemporary manuscript, "no difference in opinion shall alienate their affections any more" — roughly how the Boston church itself had managed to hold together as long as it did. Davenport preached the final sermon; he called upon all assembled to endeavor to live in Christian unity, even in the absence of unanimity of opinion. Cotton later told an English audience that one of the glories of a New England synod was that if not all the participants could come to an agreement, all the parties could nonetheless agree "without disunion of affection, or disturbance of the Churches peace. . . not to *condemn*, nor to *despise one another in differences of weaknesse.*"

This outcome, unity of a sort through an undesired diversity, appears to have been the achievement of a centrist group, probably spearheaded by Davenport and Winthrop. According to one observer, Governor Winthrop, who had no official role, took an extremely active part in ensuring that the synod was able to reach as amicable a conclusion as it did. He silenced "passionate and impertinent speeches," regularly called for scriptural references, and would adjourn the assembly when he saw "heat and passion." As a result, "jarring and dissonant opinions, if not reconciled, yet are covered." Winthrop saved the ministers from themselves. That was no small achievement. Clearly, a failed synod would have had grave consequences in Massachusetts, and there is no telling how it would have played into the debates between English Congregationalists and Presbyterians in the 1640s, as the synod's outcome was the only evidence the Congregationalists had to counter the widespread assumption that their system could not police itself.

But since the final agreement amounted to little more than an agreement not to condemn and despise each other, it was a fragile one. Cotton's party had effectively had its unity broken, as its members were well aware. Yet the most determined of Cotton's opponents had not had their way at the synod, either, and they, too, were left dissatisfied. Shepard continued to express deep mistrust of Cotton's theology and of Cotton himself. Hooker, the moderator, was no less dissatisfied. He scarcely waited until he returned to Connecticut before ripping into the compromise theological statement. Weld, when describing the synod to an English audience seven years later, could not bring himself to mention that it ended with a theological accommodation. Winthrop, in his usual irenic vein, wrote in his journal that the synod had "concluded so comfortably in all love, etc." But he himself would soon show the limits of his "love." There is evidence aplenty to suggest that Cotton's party were not the only ones who departed the synod concerned that heaven had excessively accommodated hell — an inauspicious omen for the return of Massachusetts's peace.

CHAPTER 7

Bottomless Revelations

Fall 1637

In theory, the synod should have ended the need for state intervention. It had declared Wheelwright and radicals like Hutchinson wrong
to have accused the ministers of teaching a covenant of works, and it
had condemned their "errors." That settled, the saints could return
to their unity and mutual love, as policed by the individual churches'
disciplinary processes: vigilant watch over members, private conferences, and, when necessary, trials.

But there was no agreement about what exactly the synod's final
theological statement meant nor over what constituted a proper pace
for bringing radicals and disaffected supporters of Wheelwright back
into harmony with the other churches. Cotton showed no urgency
about pushing the process of reconciliation, although he was trying to
persuade an implacably furious Wheelwright to leave the colony voluntarily. Perhaps Cotton felt somewhat guilty over how far he had
backtracked. Winthrop, however, writing for an English audience soon
thereafter, complained that the synod made little impact on Boston.
Wheelwright in Mount Wollaston, he said, preached "after his former
manner" — but he preached against errors there, claimed Cotton in
response. Hutchinson continued to hold her meetings, Winthrop complained, in spite of the synod's condemnation of them — we never
caught her saying anything heretical, Cotton answered. She and others continued to walk out whenever Wilson preached — they claimed
that female necessities required their departure, said Cotton.

The opponents of "Mr. Cotton's party" were jittery, not to say paranoid. Cotton's suspiciously leisurely pace was to them an unaffordable
luxury. According to Winthrop, Bostonians, far from being humbled
by the synod, "boasted" of how a "fitter opportunity" would come their
way "upon the return of some of their chiefe supporters." This was
certainly a reference to Vane (whom Winthrop never mentioned by

name to his English audience). How widespread talk of Vane's return was we have no way of knowing, and what Winthrop's allies like Shepard were doing to keep controversy stirred up has left no documentary trace. We do know that Hooker in Connecticut, writing a note to Winthrop after the synod, urged a "secret and suddayne" and "resolute and uncontrolable" attack on the "adversary."

The synod had explained God's word, but with lack of immediate disciplinary follow-through. Now the General Court, following Hooker's suggestion, "took courage," as Shepard later put it, and asserted the disciplinary muscle of the government in a more forceful manner. The legal and political struggle that had been initiated with Wheelwright's trial in the spring was about to come to an end. With Vane gone and Cotton uneasily neutralized, the colony's fragile government could finally bring Anne Hutchinson and others to trial.

The General Court convened in Shepard's Newtowne meetinghouse on November 2. Winthrop and whoever else was in on the planning meant to prosecute the people they considered the ringleaders in the recent agitation. They intended the trials to result either in repentance and acknowledgment of the Court's authority or in punitive consequences, including banishment. The Wheelwright petition formed the basis for the prosecutions, reasonably enough. Its tone would have been unacceptable to any English governing body, and the synod undercut its religious arguments. As will be seen, the prosecutors had a Court strongly sympathetic to their intentions, but one that was by no means a rubber stamp. It is unfortunate that for accounts of the court's proceedings up to Hutchinson's trial we have only Winthrop's journal and a narrative he wrote that winter. His depictions are surely one-sided and downplay disagreements among the Court's members, but since the polemical stakes were relatively low up to the time of Hutchinson's trial, he can be taken as roughly reliable.

Winthrop is certainly reliable in his depictions of Boston church members still seething over the treatment that Wheelwright and his allies had received and of a General Court out of sympathy with the Bostonians' belligerent behavior. When the Court's session commenced, one of Boston's deputies, William Coddington, demanded in vain that Wheelwright's conviction and the immigration order be repealed. The Court then voted to remove Boston deputy William Aspinwall for signing the Wheelwright petition. Boston deputy John Coggeshall immediately spoke up in defense of both Aspinwall and the petition, and the Court removed him as well. Aspinwall and Coggeshall were the Boston messengers who had stormed out of the synod when Cotton had discouraged them from defending "errors." Only Cotton's intervention prevented the Boston town meeting from electing them again to the General Court. One of the two replacements the town meeting chose had also signed the petition and was dismissed. The Bostonians did not replace him, but, said Winthrop, "that contempt the Court let passe."

With its membership settled, the Court began its judicial action against the Bostonians. Wheelwright's sentencing hearing was the first and the longest of any, including Hutchinson's. It consisted of three days of little more than mutual head banging, gauging from Winthrop's brief account. Wheelwright was finally given the opportunity to leave the colony in the spring, if he would not preach in the interim. Upon his refusal, the Court ordered him to leave in fourteen days. The Court next tried the two dismissed deputies, Coggeshall and Aspinwall. Like Wheelwright, they were defiant, defending both Wheelwright's doctrine and the Wheelwright petition. Aspinwall was sentenced to banishment and ordered to depart by the end of March. Coggeshall was only disenfranchised, perhaps because he did not actually sign the petition. The Court warned him, however, that if he disturbed the public peace, he, too, would be banished.

Hutchinson's trial was next. For its details, we are fortunate to be able to rely on anonymous notes as well as Winthrop. The notes, although incomplete, provide a much fuller, much more conflicted picture of the Court's proceedings than does Winthrop and bring out more clearly Hutchinson's sharp intelligence and forceful personality. Her trial is usually analyzed and interpreted in isolation, which is heavily misleading, but it differed from the previous trials in one crucial way. By its end, Hutchinson had provided her opponents with the raw materials for a highly convenient rewriting of the entire controversy, one that has shaped much of the subsequent historiography.

Winthrop began by laying out the prosecution's case. The fundamental charge was sedition: she had been "one of those who hath troubled the peace of the commonwealth and churches." More specifically,

Hutchinson had a "great share" of responsibility for "promoting and divulging" the opinions that had caused the recent troubles; she was joined in "affinity and affection" with those the Court had already censured; she had slandered the ministers of Massachusetts; and she had continued to hold her meetings even after the synod had condemned them. As in a church disciplinary hearing, Winthrop told Hutchinson that the Court had called her to either convince her of her errors or, failing that, "take such course that you may trouble us no further." Winthrop closed his address by asking Hutchinson "whether you do not justify Mr. Wheelwright's sermon and the petition."

Winthrop's question was an invitation to self-incrimination, one that the previous defendants had belligerently taken up by defending Wheelwright. But as was appropriate for a woman, Hutchinson had stayed out of the public debates in the colony, and she was not going to enter them now. "I hear no things laid to my charge," she replied. In fact, she was on stronger ground than those already convicted. Their convictions had stemmed from public acts: preaching, statements in the General Court, the signing of a "seditious" petition. Hutchinson had done none of these, as she pointed out to Winthrop. Winthrop argued back that though she may not have committed overt acts, she had "harboured" and "countenanced" those who had. She was therefore in effect a coconspirator: "If you countenance those that are transgresors of the law you are in the same fact." Hutchinson replied that all she had done was entertain them, not conspire with them. Winthrop invoked the Fifth Commandment's injunction to honor one's parents, a standard justification for deference to rulers during this period. He then told Hutchinson that those who entertained persons who had dishonored the magistrates dishonored the magistrates themselves. Hutchinson responded that Winthrop's argument only applied "if I entertain them, as they have dishonoured their parents." In other words, she had not entertained them in connection with their quarrels with the magistrates. Winthrop replied that she put honor upon them by "countenancing them above all others." Hutchinson replied, "I may put honor upon them as the children of God and as they do honor the Lord."

The drift of the trial notes indicates that Hutchinson had effectively pushed Winthrop into a corner. He was on the verge of having to argue that anyone who "entertained" John Wheelwright and the petition signers, a list that would include most of the Boston congregation and John Cotton, deserved trial. To extricate himself, he tried for the only time during Hutchinson's trial to invoke patriarchal control: "We do not mean to discourse with those of your sex but only this: you do adhere unto them and do endeavour to set forward this faction and so you do dishonour us." Hutchinson ignored his patriarchal authority and replied, "I do acknowledge no such thing, neither do I think that I ever put any dishonour upon you."

Winthrop, stymied, dropped the charge and moved on to Hutchinson's conventicles. He and Hutchinson engaged in much back-and-forth about the legitimacy of these and about her right as a woman to lead them. Winthrop finally claimed that Hutchinson, with her regular and well-attended conventicles, had in effect set up a public ministry, which she as a woman should not have done. Hutchinson acknowledged that if she had been teaching in public it would have been wrong, just as she agreed that it would have been wrong had she honored the "faction" in any dishonoring of the magistrates. She denied, however, that her conventicles constituted a public ministry, for she did not teach men in them. While Winthrop could see no validity in Hutchinson's denial, recent historians have explored the ways in which her conventicles, like her nursing and attendance at births, were a logical extension, as Amanda Porterfield has put it, of "the conventional Puritan pattern of diffused mothering." As such, they were appropriate to a woman of Hutchinson's age and social status (at least in Hutchinson's mind). Behavior that Winthrop identified in masculine terms as public, Hutchinson identified in feminine terms as private.

With Hutchinson refusing to acknowledge that she had done anything wrong with her meetings, Winthrop again found himself making dangerously general assertions: "We see not that any should have authority to set up any other exercises besides what authority hath already set up." He was on the verge of declaring puritan conventicles illegal, just as the persecuting bishops of England had done. This was an uncomfortable corner for a puritan to find himself stuck in, the more so since they were common practice in Massachusetts; was Hutchinson being sincere or extremely clever when she then invited him, in a roomful of veterans of Laudian purges, to put down her meetings "by authority"? Another magistrate, Simon Bradstreet, spoke up and tried to stop both of them from making a football of the women's meetings. He asked, did Hutchinson make her offer because the law required her to do so? Hutchinson replied it was a "free will offering." Bradstreet said, in a rebuttal to the thrust of Winthrop's argument, that he did not regard women's meetings as unlawful. Winthrop left this whole exchange out of his report to England, which, if a deliberate omission, showed good judgment—godly magistrates did not suppress the gatherings of the saints.

Winthrop was having a hard time moving from common knowledge—Hutchinson was clearly a central member of the "faction" that the Court had already determined was seditious—to a convictable offense. Hutchinson parried his first charge; she and Bradstreet had shut off his clumsy attempt to get at her via her conventicles. How the trial would have turned out had he continued to direct it, we will never know, for at this point Deputy Governor Dudley stepped in. He had a solid legal background and, as a manager who made the debt-ridden estates of the Earl of Lincoln profitable, perhaps a ruthless one.

Dudley stayed on the theme of Hutchinson's conventicles briefly, but no more successfully than Winthrop. He then moved on to the charge of slandering the ministers. After a few questions, Dudley scored the first prosecution hit. He accused Hutchinson of saying that none of the ministers except Cotton were able ministers of the New Testament. Hutchinson replied that if she had ever said that, she proved it by God's word. She thereby acknowledged a statement similar to the ones for which Wheelwright and Greensmith had already been convicted. The note taker wrote "*Court.* Very well, very well," to indicate the murmurs that ran through the room. Six ministers, professing reluctance to testify, then presented their version of the conference they had had with Hutchinson the previous October. Hutchinson freely acknowledged that she had said that their way of teaching assurance of salvation, if it was a way at all, was a "way to hell."

Hutchinson had only one significant objection to the substance of the ministers' account. As with Winthrop's questions about the Wheelwright petition and her meetings, she denied that her conversation with the ministers constituted part of the public debate in the colony. Whatever she said at the ministers' meeting came out very reluctantly and after much more urging by the ministers than they indicated. It was a private conversation, and the ministers had no business making it public. Moreover, her most defamatory statements, she claimed, occurred only in one-on-one, obviously private situations. She said that Wilson had a record of the meeting that would show that "many things are not so as is reported."

Most of the Court, however, seemed not to regard her public/private distinction or the degree to which the ministers urged her to speak as relevant to the case. It was the substance of what she said that concerned them. Probably a year previously, before the public turbulence, they would have been more sympathetic to her position, which was a moral defense, not a strictly legal one. Winthrop concluded this day's work by noting that they had labored to bring Hutchinson to acknowledge the error of her ways, and that she should consider it overnight and attend the Court in the morning.

Winthrop began the next morning by announcing that it had been plainly proved that Hutchinson had indeed said what she had been accused of saying about the ministers, and "this was spoken not as was pretended out of private conference." Perhaps because his first accusations had gotten nowhere, he reiterated a doctrinal charge that Dudley had brought up the previous day: that Hutchinson had said the letter of the scripture held forth a covenant of works was "offered to be proven by probable grounds." He allowed anyone to speak, if anyone had anything to say, but he clearly regarded the case as settled.

Hutchinson responded by dropping a large procedural wrench into the trial. She had evidently received legal counsel the night before, and she informed the Court that she wanted the ministers to give their testimony under oath. They were witnesses in their own cause, she claimed, meaning that they had brought an accusation that they had been defamed, but they had not provided any witnesses to support it. English trials at this time required prosecution witnesses to be sworn; to be witnesses, the ministers had to take oaths. The question of her reluctance to speak was the issue she wanted them sworn for, not for the substance of what she may have said to them.

Hutchinson touched a tender point with her demand that the ministers swear. The ministers throughout the controversy had tried to avoid involving themselves directly in adversarial proceedings. They preferred to present themselves as disinterested protectors of God's truth and conciliators. They would not name names in the pulpit; they had not been willing to bring formal charges against Hutchinson to the Boston church; they had worked behind the scenes at Wheelwright's trial, but when they did finally accuse him openly, they accompanied their accusations with expressions of fraternal concern; on the first day of Hutchinson's trial they stressed that they testified reluctantly. Now Hutchinson presented them simply as self-interested mortals pushing their own cause. Winthrop, understanding the larger issue she raised, immediately objected that the ministers had been unwilling to speak, except that it was "the cause of the whole country" and required by the "glory and honour of God."

Hutchinson, however, had triggered a wave of unease on the Court. Court secretary Nowell warned that there was discontent abroad that the ministers had broadcast things spoken in private. "Many" members of the Court said that they were not satisfied that the ministers testified without an oath, although the notes do not give their reasons. The only individual the note taker recorded explaining himself was Assistant Israel Stoughton, who had previously clashed with Winthrop about Winthrop's legal arbitrariness. Stoughton was not concerned for Hutchinson herself but about the need for Winthrop to observe proper legal forms. He said he was satisfied that the ministers spoke the truth, but that the "way of justice" required an oath "in this as in all other things." Winthrop reluctantly agreed to swear the ministers "that all may be satisfied."

Some members of the Court opposed the decision to make the ministers swear. One deputy cautioned that swearing to God was "of a high nature" and that it would dishonor God to have the ministers take an oath unless there was a controversy (in the New Haven colony, more severely puritan than even Massachusetts, the magistrates treated oaths so seriously that they rarely gave them). Hutchinson announced that there was indeed now a controversy, for she had witnesses of her own who would contradict the ministers.

With opinion in the Court running against them, the ministers began to acquiesce to Hutchinson's demand. Eliot, however, said that he would testify under oath, but only after he had heard the witnesses Hutchinson wanted to call, a reversal of the usual procedure, in which prosecution witnesses testified first. Dudley bluntly told the ministers that "if the country will not be satisfied you must swear." But probably to relax them, he decided to do as Eliot requested and call the defense witnesses first: Coggeshall, Leverett, and Cotton.

Those witnesses could do little to help Hutchinson (defense witnesses did not swear at this time). Coggeshall clammed up when the minister Hugh Peters snapped at him for questioning his testimony. Elder Leverett stressed that the ministers vehemently urged Hutchinson to speak, but that point was not of great concern to the Court. Cotton said he did not remember Hutchinson saying all that she was accused of, but he also acknowledged not paying attention to the entire conversation. Court members repeatedly announced that they were not swayed by the defense witnesses' testimony. Winthrop was probably reflecting the general sentiment in the room when he later wrote in his journal that the charge had been "clearly proved against her, though she sought to shift it off."

Perhaps now realizing that a conviction was inevitable, Hutchinson made a critical decision. With nothing to lose, she would drop her feminine reserve and address the Court as openly and defiantly as had the previous defendants and as her father had answered the bishop of London fifty-nine years earlier. She was driven, I imagine, by a fierce anger directed to many objects: the ministers who had betrayed a confidential conversation; the Court that was letting them get away with it; and, collectively, the enemies of the gospel who were persecuting her after she had made the sacrifice of an Atlantic crossing.

"If you please to give me leave, I shall give you the [foundation] of what I know to be true [about the ministers]," she told the Court. Winthrop later claimed that he tried to discourage her digression, but seeing her determination (and perhaps sensing opportunity), he allowed her to continue. She spoke of her fast day in England and how the Lord had sent her scriptures that showed her how to discern among the voices of Christ, Moses, John the Baptist, and Antichrist in ministers. She knew in her conscience what she said was true, and if the court condemned her for it, she committed herself to the Lord. Secretary Nowell, probing the source of her confidence, asked her how she knew that it was the Spirit who revealed this to her. Hutchinson replied by asking him how Abraham knew that it was God who commanded him to sacrifice his son, and she revealed that she had access to what she termed "immediate revelations."

Hutchinson then plunged on with her speech. She explained how

she had once been led aside into a covenant of works, how she had become confident of her revelations, and how they had brought her to
New England. She then informed the Court that she had been fore-
told, via Daniel 6, that she would experience her own lion's den and
emerge from it unharmed, through God's power. On the other hand,
she warned her persecutors, "You do as much as in you lies to put the
Lord Jesus Christ from you, and if you go in this course you begin you
will bring a curse upon you and your posterity, and the mouth of the
Lord hath spoken it." As members of the Court tried to follow her
scripture texts, she defiantly closed by paraphrasing Hebrews 11:27:
"But now having seen him which is invisible I fear not what man can
do unto me."

Hutchinson's speech must have been an extraordinary bravura per-
formance. Roger Williams had threatened divine vengeance on the
Court, and the Wheelwright petitioners implied it. None of them,
however, claimed a revelation as their authority, and neither Williams
nor the petitioners made their threat openly before the Court.
Winthrop asked her if she expected, like Daniel, to be delivered by a
miracle. Hutchinson replied that she would be delivered by the Lord's
providence (i.e., God's control of ordinary events: presumably the
providence involved the return of Vane — six months later she still
expressed the hope he would be appointed governor-general).

Assistant Endicott could not resist asking Cotton what he thought
of Hutchinson's extraordinary prediction. He and others in the room
must have been stunned by Cotton's answer: revelations by the word
of scripture and according to the word of scripture were possible, and
if Hutchinson did not expect to be delivered by a miracle but only by
a wonderful providence, he could not bear witness against it. Cotton's
response suggests just how tenuous his reconciliation with the Massachusetts authorities was, as might his willingness to appear as a defense witness in the first place. Perhaps at the moment, Cotton was
not totally averse to the idea of Vane returning as governor-general.
Winthrop repeatedly had to deflect indignant Court members from
pursuing Cotton, whom Winthrop was trying to cultivate, not crush.

Winthrop wanted to keep the focus on Hutchinson not least because he recognized that she had just handed the prosecution two substantial gifts. The first was that she had significantly simplified its task.
She had voluntarily started to expound her singular ideas about what

was wrong with the preaching of the ministers in a public forum, and she closed with a threatening speech both seditious and in contempt of court. As Winthrop later wrote to England, Hutchinson had been stonewalling the Court every step of the way in the trial, "putting matters on proof and then quarrelling with the evidence." Now she had just "freely and fully discovered herself."

The second gift was that she had dramatically shared with men from all over the colony her predilection for revelations. Since there has been confusion among scholars of Hutchinson on this point, it should be stressed that Hutchinson did not dig a pit for herself simply because she prophesied from scripture verses. The legitimacy of revelations about the future, however, was contested in puritan circles, with their acceptability at best being dependent on who had them, what context they had them in, and whose interests they served. Ministers always cited scripture verses while warning their audiences of God's impending wrath, but Hutchinson's judges took for granted that scripture verses could not possibly be correctly interpreted to mean that someone like Hutchinson was under divine protection and that God would destroy them. Hutchinson was obviously self-, and probably satanically, deluded. "Bottomlesse revelations, as either came without any word [of scripture], or without the sense of the word," summed up Winthrop precisely when explaining Hutchinson to his English audience.

Moreover, Hutchinson made her case even worse by claiming her revelations were immediate. The word "immediate" was a slippery one. According to both Wheelwright and Cotton, when the Holy Spirit communicated a meaningful scripture text to a person's mind, the result could be called an immediate revelation. It was via scripture verses that Hutchinson seems to have experienced her revelations. But "immediate" could mean without the medium of the scriptures altogether, as the anabaptists of Münster, their familist offspring, and perhaps already a few people in Massachusetts meant it. It could signal the end of the Bible as the foundational source of religious truth, a result that Shepard had been arguing from the pulpit for months was the logical destination of Cotton's teachings. It could also signal the end of all moral restraint, as well as the need for ministers or authorities of any kind, as people did whatever their divine voices told them to.

As Winthrop listened to Hutchinson speak of her revelations, he realized that she had provided an important new way to understand

Massachusetts's current troubles: they were entirely her fault. She had been teaching the godly to look to immediate (and self-evidently perverse) revelations and not to the ministers for guidance, and this, Winthrop announced to the Court, was the "root of all the mischief." The Court agreed. Dudley drew a comparison between Hutchinson and Münster. Winthrop announced he was persuaded that Hutchinson's revelations were delusions, and the entire Court, the notes record, "but some two or three ministers," cried out, "We all believe it—we all believe it." As members of the Court continued to denounce Hutchinson and the "cursed fountain" of her revelations, Winthrop moved to ratify this consensually developed, monocausal explanation of Massachusetts's recent disruptions. He asked "if therefore it be the mind of the court, looking at [Hutchinson] as the principal cause of all our trouble, that they would now consider what is to be done with her."

When the trial started, Winthrop described Hutchinson, accurately, as one of those who had troubled the peace of the commonwealth and churches; now she was the ringleader. Her ascent was rapid but predictable. It had been rumored for at least a year that a sinister conspiracy of heretics had been plotting the ruin of Massachusetts, and fear that revelations and familism, the products of Münster, were at the bottom of Massachusetts's troubles had been one of the reasons those troubles got so intense. The Münster rebellion had been led by a savage prophet, King John, and such a figure was all that was needed to make the Massachusetts puzzle complete. Hutchinson, with her revelations, had just provided it. Given Protestant history, Hutchinson the prophet and conventicle leader provided at least as compelling an explanation for what Massachusetts had been through as did Vane the Machiavellian politician. As will be shown, she was also a much more useful one.

Hutchinson's conviction was delayed when assistant Stoughton, still concerned with legal procedures, again raised the issue of sworn witnesses. Hutchinson deserved banishment, he said, but since she had requested those witnesses, he could not formally condemn her without them. Three ministers were sworn and testified, while the Boston deputies peppered the proceedings with futile objections. Stoughton announced he was satisfied, and Winthrop moved for a vote for banishment on the grounds of "these things that appear before us." The entire Court but the Boston deputies and one abstainer voted for conviction. Winthrop ordered her banished and in the meantime imprisoned. "I desire to know wherefore I am banished," Hutchinson replied, a reasonable enough request, given the vagueness of Winthrop's summary, at least as the note taker took it down. The notes stop with Winthrop's haughty response: "The court knows wherefore and is satisfied."

Secretary Nowell, however, did not allow himself Winthrop's breeziness when summarizing the proceedings in the Court records. Hutchinson had been summoned, he wrote, for "traduceing [slandering] the ministers and their ministry in this country" (Nowell omitted the unsuccessful charges). The Court found her guilty because she willingly confessed to that accusation and, to top it off, gave a speech that was both seditious and in blatant contempt of court. Or, as he phrased it, "she declared voluntarily her revelations for her ground, & that shee should be delivered & the Court ruined, with their posterity, & thereupon was banished." Scholars often argue that Hutchinson's conviction was somehow arbitrary and extralegal. A complex political process was necessary to bring her into court, and by the time she got there, the assistants and the representatives of the freemen of Massachusetts broadly agreed that the behavior and opinions of Wheelwright and his supporters constituted offenses. However, Hutchinson had a real trial, by the rough-and-tumble, disorderly standards of a period in which no speech had automatic legal protection and in which, as the English legal historian Cynthia Herrup has put it, cases were decided through a mixture of "prejudice, legal rules, and common sense." The poorly supported charges failed, and the others were amply substantiated; they could have been offenses in England. Whether a trial run by a defunct corporation carrying on in defiance of the king had any legal standing is another question altogether.

In spite of all the attention it gets from scholars, Hutchinson's trial was not nearly as important as her brother-in-law's to the free grace controversy itself. Wheelwright's opponents had to scramble to get a conviction, but by the time of Hutchinson's trial, her prosecutors did not have to work to make the Court unsympathetic to her. The result of Wheelwright's trial was months of protracted political clashes, plans to trump the local government's authority with that of the king's, and the attempted mass emigration of the Boston church. Hutchinson's conviction produced no threat to appeal to the king and no major shifts in the makeup of the General Court. A rump of the Boston congregation was already planning to leave. The men of Boston did not petition the General Court on behalf of Hutchinson (nor anyone else convicted in November), nor did the women, as they would twelve years later for the midwife Alice Tilly. As a political struggle, the controversy, with the exception of some mopping up, was effectively over by the time of Hutchinson's trial, even if the Court declared ex post facto that her newly discovered revelations carried the sole responsibility for that struggle.

What the outcome of Hutchinson's trial did provide was an important opportunity for a highly convenient reinterpretation of the entire controversy. Winthrop exploited that opportunity to the full in the account of the November trials he sent to England shortly thereafter. There he claimed that the disruptions in the colony were entirely Hutchinson's fault. They stemmed from her intention to "disclose and advance her master-piece of immediate revelations," which he elaborated at length, and they would have resulted in "the utter subversion both of Churches and civill state" had not so many elders and magistrates stayed "free from the infection." Winthrop had already explained to his readers that Wheelwright's fast-day sermon was the source of all the colony's troubles. Now he informed them that Wheelwright, who may have never backed down from a confrontation in his life, got the courage to give this sermon from Hutchinson. Hutchinson, he announced, was the "head" of a faction. Thanks to her, there was no need for him to explore the extended string of mutual provocations that resulted in the banishment of a minister like Wheelwright; no need to even raise the delicate issues of Vane and Cotton, thank heaven; and certainly no need to dwell on incendiary preachers like Shepard — no need, in short, to disturb anyone in his audience by suggesting anything problematic about the Massachusetts establishment or saying anything disrespectful of Vane.

One would have no hint from Winthrop, nor from the many historians who have derived their interpretations from his account, that seven months later, Thomas Shepard, no less simplistically, would be blaming the confusion of the free grace controversy not on Hutchinson but on Vane, in whose hands Hutchinson was but one of a number of pawns. Hutchinson would be dead within six years on the American frontier, while Vane's star in the English government was steadily rising — Winthrop made a sensible choice to blame the entire controversy on Hutchinson.

The scholar Bryce Twister has recently argued that historians who do not make Hutchinson and her gender the central issues in the free grace controversy "figuratively reenact in twentieth-century historical reconstructions of antinomianism the seventeenth-century disavowal of Hutchinson." That argument, however, although reflecting a common sentiment, has it precisely backward. The authorities made Hutchinson the central figure in the controversy as a critical part of the process of disavowing her. For scholars to then focus on Hutchinson's gender, if at the expense of neglecting her considerable skills as a creative and polemical biblical exegete, takes the disavowal of her far past what Winthrop and his brethren attempted. The enemies of Cotton's party certainly regarded Hutchinson as a major player in the disruptions that had climaxed in the "sedition" of the previous spring, rightfully so, and their horror at her revelations was genuine, as was the anger of at least some of them at having to match wits with a woman. But it is safe to assume that all of them regarded Vane as a greater and more dangerous threat while he was in Massachusetts. His shadow hung over the November trials and would continue to hang over Massachusetts for another year or more. Wheelwright, for large swaths of the controversy, was probably out in front of Hutchinson as someone whom at least the clerics hated — a professional traitor, as well as a heretic — and it was the hatred of the clerics for Wheelwright that unleashed the political strife that brought Hutchinson to trial. Attitudes toward Cotton presumably varied wildly.

The Court's final action before adjourning for a week was to allow Samuel Hutchinson to remain in the colony until after the winter, which at this early date was already proving severe. When the Court reconvened, it called in the men whom it considered the most important Wheelwright petition signers. The first ones who came in defended the petition and were disenfranchised and fined. Others, reading the writing on the wall, asked contritely that their names be taken off the petition. Repentance and recognition of the Court's authority being the point of the exercise, Winthrop wrote benignly that their request was "easily granted, and their offense with a loving admonition remitted."

The Court adjourned until November 20, but not before giving official recognition to the tireless labors of Shepard. It decided that the college for ministers it was planning would be located in Newtowne in recognition of "the vigilancy of Mr. Shepard . . . for the deliverance of all the flocks which our Lord had in the wilderness." The college would shortly be named Harvard, and Newtowne renamed Cambridge.

———

There may have been a consensus in the colony that the Court proceeded with justice in its trials, but that consensus did not penetrate very far into Boston itself. Margaret Winthrop wrote her husband a remarkable letter around November 15. They had a loving and tender marriage, but in her letter, Margaret wrestled between patriarchal deference to him and the anger that so many in Boston shared about the Court's proceedings: "Sad thougts posses my sperits, and I cannot repulce them which makes me unfit for any thinge wondrine what the lord meanes by all these troubles amounge us . . . I finde in my selfe a ferce spiret, and a tremblinge hart, not so willinge to submit to the will of god as I desyre. Thear is a time to plant and a time to pul up that which is planted, which I could desyre mite not be yet." "The lord knoweth what is best, and his wil be done," Margaret dutifully closed her letter.

Others in Boston did not attempt to bury their anger. Winthrop recorded in his journal that many members of the Boston church argued with the elders that he should be disciplined, finally. In order to prevent "a public disorder," Winthrop addressed the congregation after the Court had finished its business. Had the congregation attempted to try him, he told them, he would have first checked with the General Court and the other ministers to see if he should cooperate. In any event, he knew that the church could not inquire into Court proceedings. Nonetheless, he would willingly explain why he had spearheaded the prosecutions of his fellow church members. It was obvious that his opponents were at odds with the rest of the country. Their remaining in Massachusetts was incompatible with public peace, and so "they must be sent away." This was a man offering neither concessions nor apologies as he spoke to a room full of the friends and relatives of the three persons banished. A year after he had blackballed Wheelwright, he had won, and they had lost. Winthrop saw no need to record any response from the congregation — "God is with us," as he wrote back to his wife. "It is the Lords work, and it is marvellous in our eyes," he wrote to his brethren in England. Winthrop was not yet aware that Hutchinson had only begun the behavior that would give her a preeminence in the annals of American dissenters.

CHAPTER 8

A Notorious Imposter

Winter 1637–1638

Snow blanketed Massachusetts from early November to late March in the dreary, cold winter of 1637–38. In these dark months, the Massachusetts authorities finally managed to create through their repression the implacable heretics that they had long been hunting, and the consensual mechanisms that had more or less held the Boston church together broke down. Hutchinson's extraordinarily creative, brazen, and shifty behavior in this period helped to drive that breakdown, and it prompted Winthrop to give her the sobriquet that has subsequently graced any number of book and article titles: the American Jezebel, equal of the wicked biblical queen.

Prior to the November trials, radicals like Hutchinson muted their opinions and/or presented them as "questions." They did so both to protect themselves from retaliation and to maintain harmony with Wheelwright and Cotton in the struggle against "legalists" like Shepard. The trials and banishments, however, broke their tenuous ties to clerical puritanism, even of Cotton and Wheelwright's variety. That November Wheelwright found himself angrily attacked by one of his listeners while preaching his farewell sermon at Mount Wollaston. Wheelwright, the listener charged, preached "Antichristianisme," like the other ministers. The listener went on to recite the most extreme, familist-drenched series of theological propositions yet recorded in Massachusetts. Other radicals followed Hutchinson's lead and vigorously espoused immediate revelations. "Had this sect gone on awhile," summarized Edward Johnson, "they would have made a new Bible."

The General Court reacted strongly when it reconvened on November 20. It ordered all the colony's gunpowder and ammunition removed from Boston to Newtowne and Roxbury, a logical, if hysterical, preface to the proclamation it then made. "The opinions & revelations of Mr Wheelwright & Mrs Hutchinson," the Court claimed, "have seduced & led into dangerous errors many of the people heare in Newe England." The Court justly suspected that "some revelation" might produce a repetition of Münster with "some sudden irruption upon those that differ from them in judgment." To prevent that bloody result, the Court declared that any Wheelwright petition signers who would not recant, as well as some other men "who had been chief stirrers in these contentions," had to hand in their weapons and ammunition.

The Court ordered seventy-five men disarmed out of an English population of roughly eight thousand. This was a small number, but fifty-eight of those men came from Boston. Thus, the magistrates and people's representatives with the most fearful imaginative lives might have pictured up to a sixth of the adult males of the colony's chief town as ready to reenact the bloody apocalyptic reign of King John of Münster under the guidance of Wheelwright and Hutchinson (perhaps upon Vane's return). That alarm might seem paranoid, but it should not be underestimated how culturally normative fear of Münster was. Deputy Governor Dudley, while in England, once shared a bed in an inn with a man who started talking about his revelations. Dudley's thoughts turned to Münster, and, dreading being murdered in his sleep, he moved to another room.

————

Despite, or perhaps because of, the Court's continued flexing of its muscles, Hutchinson, under house arrest in Roxbury, grew both bolder and more blatant in her speculation. Orthodox Christians linked conversion to their conception of the purpose of history: the slow and painful repairing of the corruption that the Fall of man inflicted on a once-sinless human nature in the Garden of Eden. That process of healing would be complete only at the end of time with the resurrection and separation of the now-sinless physical bodies of the saints and the doomed bodies of the damned.

Hutchinson now put the finishing touches on an alternative plan for history in which human nature was at best a distraction. In the Garden of Eden, human nature was overwhelmed by the divine until Adam and Eve asserted their own wills by eating the forbidden fruit. That overwhelming happened again in conversion, and what was resurrected at the end of time were not physical bodies but spiritual ones (it has been suggested that Hutchinson's extreme devaluing of the physical body came from her intimate feminine knowledge of the pain and suffering it caused). One element of Hutchinson's scheme was that the souls of humans along with their physical bodies were wiped out at death, while a separate entity that Hutchinson called the spirit went to heaven or hell. Hutchinson's theology had extensive familist antecedents, as well as antecedents in debates among the Boston radicals. In its final form, the heresies it contained were so blatant that even Cotton noticed them.

He could hardly avoid noticing them because Hutchinson made no secret of her new opinions. She had many visitors while under house arrest and became pregnant. She not only discussed theology with her visitors but also told them that her revelations about future events (which included the destruction of the General Court) were to be believed as firmly as scripture. Hutchinson announced definitively that Christ's disciples had not been converted at Christ's death — so much for the ministers of Massachusetts. The doctrine began circulating, from Hutchinson or someone else, that the linchpin of puritan piety, the Sabbath, had no moral basis.

The mood in Massachusetts was grim: heresy growing, Vane, for all anyone knew, plotting his return, and people on both sides aggressively confrontational. "It cuts a mans hart to thinke what is intended against us," Shepard told his congregation at the end of December. "Judases to betraye us, Enemyes to assault us." The Scituate church, probably not uniquely, held a fast day for "the removeall of the Spreading opinions in the churches at the Bay, as alsoe for the preventing of any intended evill against the churches here." Radicals may have been small in number and politically neutralized, but they more than made up for this by their demoralizing visibility in the environs of the colony's chief town. Meanwhile, the winter grew so cold and snowy that there was talk of abandoning Boston for lack of access to firewood.

The growing militancy of the radicals, however demoralizing it might have been, had a positive result for Massachusetts's stability. Up to this time, Hutchinson and the other radicals had gotten along not because their sympathizers had turned "Hutchinsonian" but because the radicals had behaved in recognizably pious ways and as much as was possible kept themselves wrapped in the mantels of Cotton and

Wheelwright. Now, as they were appearing the most menacing to the authorities, they were also alienating the more moderate support networks that had protected them and given them real influence. They thereby tipped the balance of opinion against them in the congregations where they were most numerous, Roxbury and Boston, and allowed the disciplinary mechanisms of those churches finally to come into action.

Roxbury commenced its disciplinary proceedings in January. A few members were admonished. When that did not have the desired effect, five or six men were excommunicated. Some members were excommunicated for their radical beliefs, some for supporting Wheelwright and the Wheelwright petition.

Boston never regarded support for Wheelwright as an offense against church order, but the new militancy alarmed it. Cotton himself worked hard, both publicly and privately, to bring back to the orthodox fold those who had wandered too far astray. He must have been horrified and humiliated to discover that when he finally labored intensively to disabuse the radicals of their "misexpressions" and "inquiries," they often refused to give them up. He probably would have gotten more accommodating responses had he done so eighteen months earlier. The only benefit of the defiant, vocal heterodoxy for Cotton was that it allowed him to create and share the story that he used ever after to explain away his role in the recent disturbances. He had been "abused" and made the "stalking horse" of a few heretics, Winthrop recorded him explaining in January 1638, who had cloaked their heresies under the mantle of pretending to "hold nothing but what Mr. Cotton held." Just how willingly and why Cotton had made himself the stalking horse of people he now considered heretics he preferred to forget.

For two days in January the magistrates and elders of the churches met in Boston to discuss ways to combat the new opinions. The Boston elders agreed that they would try Hutchinson if they had sufficient evidence from outsiders. According to Winthrop, they thought it would be "not so orderly" if they themselves were witnesses. Perhaps they were torn between dismay at Hutchinson and continuing anger at the rough treatment Wheelwright and his supporters had gotten. A number of divines helped them out by meeting with Hutchinson in Roxbury. Shepard himself visited her three times. On his second visit, he assured Hutchinson that he did not come to entrap her, and Hutchinson, a slow learner in the ways of ministers, vigorously debated her new opinions with him. Having drawn her out, Shepard concluded that Hutchinson's "Willingness to open herselfe and to divulge her Opinions and to sowe her seed in us that are but Highway side and Straynegers to her" made her a "very dayngerous Woman." He returned a third time to "reduce her from her Errors and to bare witness against them." For good measure, he gave the Boston elders a list of her errors. Ministers Weld and Eliot also talked with Hutchinson and drew up another list of her errors. Presented with that evidence, the Boston church agreed that she should stand trial.

That trial commenced on March 15, part of a combined church and state disciplinary mopping-up action. Three days previously, the General Court had convened. It first dealt with a group of radicals and disillusioned supporters of Wheelwright who planned to form a colony on Aquidneck Island in Narragansett Bay, not far from Roger Williams's settlement of Providence. The colonists were led by William Coddington, with the Hutchinsons well represented. The Court gave the group permission to depart "to avoyde the censure of the Court." It ordered some Salem supporters of Williams out at the same time. The Court called four militia officers who had expressed sympathy for those being punished. Most offered satisfactory apologies, saying, according to Winthrop, that "they had been deceived and misled by the pretence, which was held forth, of advancing Christ." The events of the recent months had persuaded the officers that "their opinions and practices tended to disturbance and delusion." Those recantations, while given under pressure, probably reflect a general lay reevaluation of the radicals, and they help explain why Hutchinson's church trial turned out the way it did.

Church trials were more open-ended and informal than secular trials. At the same time, they were more solemn, as befitted their sacred nature. A church trial for heresy was a stage on which one of the basic issues of puritanism could be probed: ideally, Christians were of one mind in spiritual matters and followed one path to heaven, but in the diversity of the real world, how much would their community hold itself together through love and mutual toleration and how much through severity and strict doctrinal policing? Hutchinson's church trial was also a stage for a more immediate issue: dealing with the copious amounts of bad blood the free grace controversy had engendered. At the trial's center, Cotton did his best, in the face of not unwarranted skepticism, to send Hutchinson into exile not as an excommunicant but as a repentant saint. He would ultimately fail, but that failure was by no means a given.

On the first day of the proceedings, it was clear that Hutchinson's was to be no ordinary church trial. The Boston meetinghouse was full with people from all over the colony. Numerous ministers attended, including Shepard, and would have been sitting together on benches at the front. Because the Court was in session, Winthrop and Richard Bellingham, both Boston church members, were the only magistrates occupying the magistrate's bench near the ministers. John Wilson presided with the assistance of the two ruling lay elders, Thomas Oliver and Thomas Leverett. John Cotton would have been sitting with the other Boston elders. Hutchinson, also up front, perhaps had a stool to rest on. Conspicuously absent were Hutchinson's husband and chief male allies, who were among the men negotiating for their future home in Narragansett Bay ("the good providence of God so disposed" it, wrote Winthrop; one might suspect human agency as well in the timing). As with Hutchinson's civil trial, two accounts of the proceedings have survived, the notes of a Boston church member, Robert Keayne, and Winthrop's description in *Short Story*. Keayne truncated and left out material, and it is not always possible to be sure exactly what his speakers meant to say. Winthrop's account is not sympathetic to Hutchinson, and it is far shorter than Keayne's, but it appears to be basically accurate and complements Keayne in useful ways.

The trial began after Cotton's morning lecture. Elder Oliver told the assembly at Hutchinson's request that she had missed Cotton's lecture not out of contempt but because of weakness stemming from having been under long durance (pregnancy and house arrest). Elder Leverett asked the congregation to separate itself out from the rest of the audience so it could more easily express its consent or dissent from the proceedings. After the shuffling in the room had died down, he read two lists of opinions attributed to Hutchinson. The first, submitted by Shepard and the ruling elder of his church, Edmund Frost, mostly concerned her familist-derived ideas about body, soul, and

Christ. The second, from Weld and Eliot, focused mostly on her anti-nomianism. Leverett asked Hutchinson if these were her opinions.

Hutchinson answered with fierce defiance, despite her weakness and the formidable forces marshaled against her. If the opinions were hers, she replied, they were errors, but if they were Christ's, they were truth, whereupon she launched into an attack on Shepard. He came to her in private and claimed he did not intend to ensnare her. To then bring the matter to the church without "privately dealing" with her was a violation of scriptural rule. Shepard explained his visits and added that he did not know "wherein I could deale more lovingly with this your Sister than to bringe her thus before you." Hutchinson then argued that the points she had raised with Shepard were only questions about the meaning of scripture verses. Shepard responded that the "vilest Errors" were brought into churches by questions. Cotton agreed with him and requested that Hutchinson respond to each of the opinions on the lists.

The first opinion concerned Hutchinson's claim that the spirit, not the soul, was immortal. Hutchinson held to her position, despite much back-and-forth with her by Cotton, Wilson, and Winthrop. John Davenport, Cotton's houseguest, then took over debating Hutchinson. He began ominously. Davenport, like the few historians who have paid attention to Hutchinson's new doctrines, associated them with the ancient heresy of mortalism, which is understandable but not strictly accurate. Mortalism, in all its many variations, posited that self-awareness was extinguished at death, which Hutchinson did not. Orthodox Christians saw mortalism as an "eat, drink, and be merry, for tomorrow you die" invitation to sinning.

Davenport accordingly warned Hutchinson, "They that speake for the Mortalitie of the soule speake most for Licentiousnesse and sinfull Liberty." Perhaps the warning softened up Hutchinson, for Davenport soon achieved a breakthrough. He argued with her that the spirit was not an entity separate from the soul, as Hutchinson thought, but that it was the life of the soul or its bent and bias. Hutchinson exclaimed, "God by him hath given me Light." That was not to say, however, that she had been wrong before. When she called the life of the soul a separate entity, the spirit, she made only a terminological mistake, not a substantive one. She explained to the assembly, "I doe acknowledge my Expression to be Erroneous but my Judgment was not Erroneous." Some in the room, like Cotton, were pleased to see Hutchinson change her mind. Others, like John Eliot, were appalled, as Eliot said shortly, that she would dismiss "so gross and so dayngerous an opinion" as only a mistake.

Now that Hutchinson had recanted her first opinion, or rather, claimed she never really held it, Cotton moved the discussion on to her next three. These familist-derived opinions denied a resurrection of the physical body and emphasized that spiritual union with Christ in conversion was a resurrection. They also intersected with the most lurid stereotypes of familist social meltdown. If the resurrection was over after conversion, which familists held, then the institution of marriage was inevitably also over (Matthew 22:30: "In the resurrection they neither marry nor are given in marriage"), as their opponents accused them of believing (and some extremists did). Minister Peter Bulkeley asked Hutchinson if she maintained the "foule, gross, filthye and abominable opinion held by the Familists" of a sexually shared community of women? Women's good names, far more than men's, depended on their sexual propriety, and Hutchinson lashed back, comparing Bulkeley to a pharisee. Davenport and Winthrop warned her that she could not evade Bulkeley's conclusion. Elder Leverett came to Hutchinson's aid, remarking that she did not deny that some sort of body was resurrected, to which Hutchinson agreed. She gave no further ground, however, and denied that the prophets Moses, Elijah, and Enoch were taken up to heaven in their physical bodies, as the Bible indicated. Davenport's patience snapped: "These are opinions that cannot be borne." Wilson told the congregation to hold up their hands if they were convinced that Hutchinson held "gross and damnable Heresies."

A few laymen tried to defer the censure, to the displeasure of the ministers. Hutchinson was not yet convinced one way or the other, argued her son, Edward, and she should not be condemned for opinions she was not settled in (the long-standing excuse made by/for the Boston radicals). Wilson suggested that the church move to admonition, but he invited anyone else with objections to speak. Hutchinson's son-in-law Thomas Savage found a relevant scriptural precedent in the apostolic Church of Corinth, which tolerated unsound opinions, while Edward Gibbons suggested they give Hutchinson more time to be convinced. Reverend Simmes pronounced himself "much grieved" that members of the congregation would express unwillingness to proceed against Hutchinson on such a fundamental point as the resurrection of the body. He worried that if word of this reached England, "it will be one of the greatest Dishonors to Jesus Christ and of Reproach to these Churches that hath beene done since we came hither."

It was not only ministers who grew impatient and even angry with the reluctance of some brethren to forthrightly condemn heresy and incipient moral breakdown. Ruling elder Thomas Oliver and his son John, both of whom had signed the Wheelwright petition, now spoke. Thomas asked the ministers if unanimity was needed to censure when not all the members consented, or whether the dissenting members themselves could be censured. Cotton replied that if the dissenters did so only out of "natural affection," the church could proceed (Savage and Edward Hutchinson probably were acting simply out of "natural affection," since later statements of theirs suggest that they had never been as radical as Anne). John Oliver proposed that Edward Hutchinson and Savage be admonished along with Anne. The male church members silently agreed to the admonitions.

Ordinarily, Wilson, who as pastor was in charge of discipline, would have given the admonition. The ministers conferred among themselves, however, and requested that Cotton deliver it, "as one whose Wordes by the Blessinge of God may be of more Respect." Certainly, the odds were greater that Hutchinson would listen to Cotton, but at least some of the ministers probably intended this request at least in part as a hard ball to Cotton.

Cotton nimbly fielded the toss. He thanked the ministers for the care they had shown for his church. Acknowledging that he had been slow to proceed against church members, Cotton explained that this was only for want of sufficient evidence. Now that they had proceeded in a way of God, it would be a sin not to act. Cotton thereupon admonished Hutchinson's relatives. For good measure he cautioned the sisters of the congregation, "many of whom I fear have beene too much seduced and led aside by her." Hutchinson's work among the women had not been entirely bad, he said, for she had led many of them out of the snares of the covenant of works. Nonetheless, he warned the sisters to discriminate carefully between the good and bad they had received from Hutchinson and not to harden her heart against repentance by expressing sympathy for her. Cotton then addressed Hutchinson, again fulsomely and respectfully praising her many virtues and her evangelical successes. But the dishonor she brought upon herself was far greater than any previous honor. Turning to the hoary topic of familist promiscuity, Cotton had the decency to first acknowledge that he had neither heard nor suspected that Hutchinson had been unfaithful to her husband. "Yet that will follow upon it," he warned.

As Cotton started to wax eloquent on Hutchinson's coming sexual degradation ("more dayngerous Evills and filthie Uncleanness and other sins will followe than you doe now Imagine or conceive"), Hutchinson interrupted, asking for permission to speak. She was afraid that because of her weakness she would forget to make the point when Cotton was finished. Cotton granted it. "All that I would say is this," Hutchinson said, "that I did not hould any of these Thinges before my Imprisonment." Cotton acknowledged that he thought she was right. He warned her, however, that for a person of her spiritual reputation to entertain such opinions even as questions was as dangerous to others as holding them positively, an indication of the delicate dance that Hutchinson and Cotton had been doing around each other while they were perceiving each other as allies. He then finished with his admonition. Cotton emphasized again, if less luridly, the moral collapse that would follow in the wake of Hutchinson's denials of natural immortality and physical resurrection and chastised her for the "Evill that you have done to many a poore soule" and the disgrace that she brought upon her congregation.

While Cotton gave Hutchinson a mixture of praise and grave rebukes, Shepard seethed. He was furious both at Cotton's bestowing so many compliments on her and at Hutchinson's presumptuous interruption during what was supposed to be entirely a sackcloth and ashes ritual — he would still be seething a year later. As soon as Cotton was finished, Shepard voiced his displeasure. "Lest the Crowne should be set on her Head in the day of her Humiliation," he wanted to get in a word "before the Assemblie break up." He was astonished that Hutchinson would dare to interrupt Cotton in the midst of a solemn admonition (and, by implication, that Cotton would let her). He was further astonished that she claimed that she had not held any of these opinions before her imprisonment. She had told him that winter that if he had visited her earlier, she could have told him much more about union with Christ. That she could forget this made him fear greatly for the unsoundness of her heart. Reverend Eliot seconded him. Wilson, rather than have Hutchinson answer Shepard then, ended the proceedings, as it was eight o'clock. He told her to reappear in a week's time.

The final outcome of Hutchinson's trial was by no means clear at the end of the day. Hutchinson had devoted little energy to the role of repentant sinner. She challenged Shepard's right to bring charges, compared Bulkeley to a pharisee, confessed only to terminological confusion, not error, and interrupted Cotton's admonition. Yet it cannot be entirely a coincidence that while at least eight ministers were present, it was Shepard who first protested at the end of the evening. Other persons, in contrast, expressed optimism, apparently because Hutchinson had yielded at all. In his journal Winthrop claimed that "all did acknowledge the special presence of God's spirit" at the trial. The General Court, he stated, "in regard that she had given hope of her repentance," licensed her to stay at Cotton's house for Cotton and Davenport to soften her up further. Such optimism on such fairly slender grounds may give a glimpse of the community's assessment of how stiff Hutchinson's personality was.

Winthrop's optimism appeared justified when the trial resumed a week later. Hutchinson began by reading a retraction of all the errors she had been charged with, and she made no effort this time to excuse herself with a judgment/expression distinction. Moreover, she had been wrong to have prophesied the destruction of the colony, wrong to have been disrespectful to the ministers, and sorry that she had drawn people away from hearing them. Seemingly conceding the main point of the whole controversy, Hutchinson said that sanctification could indeed be evidence of justification "as it flowes from Christ and is witnessed to us by the Spirit."

Given who Hutchinson was, this was an extraordinary statement of contrition. According to Cotton, it "far exceeded the expectation of the whole congregation, which then consisted of many churches, and strangers [persons not yet belonging to a church]." After hearing her recantation, "the Assembly," according to Winthrop, "conceived hope of her repentance." Could the trial have stopped at this point, Hutchinson would have left Massachusetts a member in good standing of the Boston church and thus one of the colony's official saints.

Like some of the other exiles, she might have found herself back in Boston eventually after a suitably apologetic and deferential petition to the General Court.

But, as Wilson immediately reminded Hutchinson, she still had to answer Shepard's accusation that she had held her errors before her imprisonment. She reiterated that it was her disrespect to the ministers and magistrates at her trial that led to her errors, and she was bluntly and almost certainly falsely dismissive of Shepard's charge: "If Mr. Shephard doth conceive that I had any of these Thinges in my Minde [before the trial], than he is deceived."

Shepard quickly spoke up. He was appalled, he told the assembly, that at a time when Hutchinson should be showing nothing but abject humiliation, "she shall cast Shame upon others and say they are mistaken." Moreover, the recantation that had made such a favorable impression on others in the room left him cold. What she had just said did not sound like "true Repentance" (both Shepard and Hooker thought that Cotton had engineered the trial to protect Hutchinson). "Any Hereticke may bringe a slye Interpretation upon any of these Errors and yet hould them to their Death," Shepard warned. Specifically, when she claimed that sanctification flowed from Christ, had she really given up her old idea that our holiness was in Christ and was thus not something that transformed our own nature? Eliot echoed Shepard's concerns.

Cotton probably suspected that Shepard's concern about heresy was directed at him as well as Hutchinson. In any case, he ran interference for her, for the last time. "Sister was there not a Time," he asked Hutchinson, "when once you did hould that there was no distinct graces inherent in us but all was in Christ Jesus?" All Hutchinson had to do was say, yes, she had once denied that God gave the saints a distinct holiness of their own, and she recognized her error. That, very likely, would have been the end of the trial, let Shepard fume as he might.

But saying yes would also mean acknowledging that she had held errors before her imprisonment. For whatever reason, that was a line of humiliation Hutchinson would not cross. Instead, she fell back on her self-exculpatory tactics of the previous session. She had never really denied the reality of inherent graces (the holiness implanted in human nature by sanctification), she insisted; she had only mistaken what the word "inherent" meant until Davenport cleared it up.

Jaws dropped across the meetinghouse. A number of ministers and laity reminded her how adamantly she had denied inherent graces. Hutchinson stuck to her position, however, using the same explanation she had the previous week: "My judgment is not altered though my expression alters." It is easy enough to share in the audience's amazement. To the extent that Hutchinson's rationale can be surmised, she may have meant that she never denied that the saints had a new holiness but had labeled it incorrectly because of what she was now claiming had been an erroneous conception of what "inherent" meant. Hutchinson was probably not a person to whom conceding serious error ever came easily. She certainly would not have readily believed that ministers who had never experienced the witness of the Spirit could have known something significant about conversion that she did not. She may have also been playing by the rules of an earlier period where everyone maintained the pretense that they were all fundamentally saying the same thing, since they were all godly.

Hutchinson's audience, however, was not entirely inclined to give her the benefit of the doubt about her godliness, and though some of her opinions were recent, inherent graces had been a heated topic for the last two years. Deputy Governor Dudley, present for this session, now focused the attack, just as he had done at Hutchinson's civil trial. Like Shepard, he must have been fuming at the leniency of Cotton's admonition, and he opened with a heavy dose of sarcasm aimed as much at Cotton as at Hutchinson: "Mrs. Hutchinson's Repentance is only for Opinions held since her Imprisonment, but before her Imprisonment she was in a good Condition, and held no Error, but did a great deale of Good to many." Dudley himself, he went on, knew of no harm she had done since her imprisonment, and he saw no repentance in her. He darkly wondered out loud if she had written her statement of repentance entirely herself, but that he would "not now Inquire to." Dudley wanted the ministers to speak to the question of whether Hutchinson held errors before her imprisonment. Ministers cited relevant discussions with her, while Shepard, impatient as always, tried to bring down a summary judgment: "I thinke it is needless for any other now to speake and useless for the Case is playne, and here is Witnesses enough."

Other ministers, however, were not as ready as Shepard to excommunicate Hutchinson. They recalled more incidents when she had denied inherent graces before her imprisonment. It is hard to read the mood in a room almost four hundred years distant through imperfect trial notes, but two things seem clear. The first is that all the speakers thought Hutchinson's answer to Cotton was objectively a lie. The second is that among the speakers, all except Shepard still wanted to bring her around to admit and/or realize it herself. This was still a healing ritual, in other words, not a hanging one. The last of the ministers in this round to speak was Hugh Peters. He asked Hutchinson to search her heart for further repentance and cautioned her that he feared she was not well grounded in her catechism! Peters then asked Hutchinson to consider that she had stepped out of all the various subordinate identities she occupied — she had been a husband rather than a wife, a preacher rather than a hearer, and a magistrate rather than a subject — and she had not yet been humbled for this multiple subordination. Some scholars have seen Peters's statement as a frank expression of his anger at Hutchinson for forgetting her place as a woman. It was that in part, but two of his three categories applied to men as well as to women. The general principle of subordination to authority in a hierarchical society was what Hutchinson was forgetting, just as Vane had forgotten it when he disagreed with Peters over a year ago, in spite of what Peters told him was his youth and ignorance.

Winthrop followed Peters. He, too, seems to have been more interested in turning the trial into a teaching and healing experience than simply a punishment of Hutchinson, for he had a further request. Diverse sisters of the congregation had "builded upon her Experience," and Winthrop thought it would be "much to Gods Glory" for Hutchinson to explain what her state of salvation consisted of if it did not lie in ingrafting into Christ (being joined to Christ by faith and the Holy Spirit). After all, she had said once that a man could be ingrafted into Christ and still fall away. We have no idea what Hutchinson was making of this general skepticism about her integrity, as her voice had stopped being recorded in the notes after she offered her judgment/expression distinction.

Shepard stayed out of the questioning. He had long since decided that time spent on dialogue with Hutchinson was only time spent putting off her just deserts. Now he spoke up, all facade of restraint gone, and finally got the proceedings heading toward his desired end. They were not dealing with a visible saint, he told the assembly, whose only fault was that she held incorrect opinions and could be dealt with by admonishment. He then delivered a dreadful charge, one that he had long implied in public but had managed, barely, to avoid saying directly: Hutchinson was in all likelihood a damned sinner. They were dealing with "one that never had any true Grace in her heart and that by her own Tenet." In other words, as he had been saying all along, the only way you could argue like Hutchinson against the inherent graces of sanctification was if God had not justified you, and you had never experienced them. Hutchinson was not a misguided member of their holy community. She was a "Notorious Imposter," and her judgment/expression distinction was "a Tricke of as notorious Subtiltie as ever was held in the Church." Where Winthrop had wanted Hutchinson to explain herself for the edification of those who had been led astray by her, Shepard suggested that the same purpose would be served by excommunication. Peters more cautiously agreed that Hutchinson's repentance only for errors after her imprisonment was not satisfactory.

Whatever reservoir of patience with Hutchinson there was in the room was shallow, and the heat of Shepard's attack seems to have evaporated it among the ministers. Keayne's notes next record Wilson accusing her of being an instrument of the devil, raised up to cause divisions among them. It was now clear, he claimed, with less than impeccable logic, that all the "wofull Opinions" in the colony came from her, since an unsound foundation had to be at the bottom of an unsound building. He asked the congregation to assent to excommunicating Hutchinson. All the ministers who now spoke, by Keayne's account, agreed, although for different reasons. For Cotton, Hutchinson's refusal to admit she had been in error accomplished what her attacks on the ministers, heterodox "inquiries," and prophecy of destruction to the General Court could not; it caused him to finally wash his hands of her. He was satisfied that Hutchinson was lying, he told the assembly, and should be excommunicated. Cotton must have been appalled that Hutchinson could defile this sacred event by lying. He presumably also would have been highly irritated that she had thrown away the opportunity at rehabilitation he had worked so hard to provide her, with him sticking his neck out a great deal for her in the process. She had also thrown away the last opportunity for him to demonstrate the basic soundness of his congregation and of his own judgment over the last few years. Davenport, more overtly compassionate, addressed Hutchinson directly, the only one of the speakers to do so, saying he feared that God would not let her see her falsehood until she had benefited from the ordinance of excommunication.

Some laymen, even those who had been forthright in moving against Hutchinson the previous week, expressed discomfort with this solidified ministerial determination to expel her. Elder Oliver, instrumental in her admonishment, did not think the church would have moved with such speed. He was seconded by Elder Leverett and others.

Shepard stepped in again, alarmed that the laity were moving to give Hutchinson another admonition instead of excommunicating her. It would be against the honor of both God and the congregation, he stressed, to do anything less than excommunicate her. Someone said he consented to the church's moving against her for lying, but not for her doctrine because she had repented of that. Wilson replied that she should be excommunicated for doctrine as well, and he doubted that her repentance was sincere. Cotton, however, said only that she was being excommunicated for lying and that apostolic precedent demanded that they act immediately in such a case. Thereby, he later claimed, he "satisfyed the Scruples of some Brethren, who doubted it."

Cotton's insistent signal that he was finished with Hutchinson seems to have settled the issue, for Keayne's notes next record Wilson's motion to excommunicate her. The church gave its consent by the usual silence. The laity might not have moved so fast on their own to excommunicate her, perhaps in part because they did not share as strongly the anger of some ministers, articulated by Wilson and Peters, that Hutchinson had presumed to compete with them. Nonetheless, they did not see her punishment as unwarranted.

After a "convenient pause," Wilson pronounced the sentence of excommunication over Hutchinson and commanded her "as a leper" to leave the building. He excommunicated her not only for lying but also for doctrinal errors. This was a bit of a fast one, given the conversation beforehand, not that anyone seems to have paid much attention. The Boston church records have Hutchinson excommunicated only for lying, as do Winthrop's journal and his account to England, and as did Cotton remembering the event eight years later. An uneasy coalition of elders, magistrates, and ordinary laity — some focusing on Hutchinson, some taking shots at Cotton; some wanting to move with haste, others more carefully; some wanting punishment, others rehabilitation; some wanting purging of the community, others healing; some irate about dogma, others more willing to cut Hutchinson doctrinal slack — pushed along by Shepard and massively assisted by Hutchinson herself, agreed that their communion of visible saints could not tolerate Hutchinson, although, as Wilson's final sleight of hand shows, they might not have agreed precisely as to why.

What Hutchinson was thinking while her trial moved to its conclusion is unrecorded, but any repentance she might have worked herself into feeling probably evaporated as the church refused to buy into her judgment/expression distinction. As she left the meetinghouse, her ally Mary Dyer bravely rose up and accompanied her — Dyer was refining a piety of defiance that would get her hanged as a Quaker in the same town twenty-two years later. A person standing by the door as Hutchinson left said to her, "The Lord sanctifie this unto you," and Hutchinson replied, "Better to be cast out of the Church than to deny Christ." Winthrop claimed that after Hutchinson was excommunicated, "her spirits, which seemed before to be somewhat dejected, revived again, and she gloried in her sufferings, saying, that it was the greatest happiness, next to Christ, that ever befel her." The next day the snow that had covered the ground a foot and a half deep since the November trials began to melt.

———

Shortly thereafter, Winthrop finished his account of the free grace controversy for his English audience and ended it with a strikingly counterintuitive argument: Hutchinson's disastrous story proved that the Massachusetts church/state consensual disciplinary system worked according to divine plan. Had not Hutchinson "kept her strength and reputation, even among the people of God, till the hand of Civill Justice laid hold on her?" And did she not thereafter begin "evidently to decline and the faithfull to bee freed from her forgeries?" She cunningly tried to insinuate her way back among the saints at her church trial by her expression/judgment distinction, "yet such was the presence and blessing of God in his own Ordinance" that this "subtilty of Satan" was exposed and Hutchinson was excommunicated. The church trial itself worked to the benefit of the faithful, for Hutchinson's lying there made even more "godly hearts" realize what a fraud she was. That realization helped to knit back together the Boston church, which lay under "much infamy" and had been brought "neere to dissolution." The way state and church had worked together to defeat this larger-than-life "American Jesabel" demonstrated the "presence of God in his Ordinances when they are faithfully attended according to his holy will."

As usual, God had conceived an extremely complicated and nail-biting plot, and as usual, He had ultimately made everything work for the good of His people and to the further demonstration of His glory. Winthrop had obvious public relations reasons for putting such a positive spin on the story of Hutchinson. Nonetheless, that relentless determination to find God's plan in the chaos of human affairs permeates his journal, and there is no reason to doubt that he believed what he wrote when he changed this near catastrophe into a divinely guided, predestined triumph and vindication of Massachusetts's institutions. Winthrop's depiction of Hutchinson's downfall gives a glimpse into the foundations of the puritan confidence that made the survival of Massachusetts possible against formidable odds, many of them self-imposed.

CHAPTER 9

All One Indian

There is a curious account of Anne Hutchinson in her final days in Massachusetts. Ordered to leave the colony by the end of March, Hutchinson went to her farm at Mount Wollaston on March 28. From there she was to sail to New Hampshire with her sister-in-law Mary Wheelwright and her mother-in-law, Susan, to join Wheelwright in exile. Why that destination would even cross her mind is hard to grasp. Her husband was presumably in Aquidneck at the time. Wheelwright opposed her chief doctrine of the denial of inherent graces. He later set up his new church in a proper relationship to the churches of Massachusetts, which meant that he would not have let Hutchinson participate in the Lord's Supper until she had the sentence of excommunication lifted by the Boston church. Perhaps she was still somewhat under the sway of Davenport and Cotton and open to (relatively) orthodox guidance, such as Wheelwright would provide. Perhaps she did not want to leave the comfort and services of an ordained minister, as would be the case in her new colony.

Whatever Hutchinson was thinking, she changed her mind and went by land to Aquidneck. Ahead of her lay a truly new world. There would be no more compromises about her doctrines necessary and no more connection to a state-sponsored church and minister; the struggle with separatism that dated back at least to Hutchinson's memorable fast in England was over, thanks in part to her most bitter enemies. Early in April, Plymouth governor William Bradford wrote to Winthrop, saying he had heard that Hutchinson had retracted her confession of errors. Meanwhile, Massachusetts's godly community was left to try to patch itself together after two years of violent quarrels and the flood of what one participant later described as "Hell's Cataracts . . . of Errors."

Hutchinson was one among a sizable number of voluntary and involuntary exiles leaving Massachusetts in the spring of 1638. Over eighty men and their families went to Aquidneck, while a smaller contingent joined Wheelwright in New Hampshire. Davenport and his wealthy supporters left to establish New Haven. These demoralizing departures took place in a spring so disastrously wet and cold that the first seedlings died, and the colony faced the possibility of famine. The threat of a governor-general hung in the air. All in all, the colonists had good reason to think that God was very angry at them.

But the spring warmed up and the second planting thrived. Winthrop was reelected governor, and that summer saw the largest immigration from England to date. Meanwhile, King Charles had provoked his presbyterian Scottish subjects into rebellion by attempting to force Laud's reforms of the Church of England on them. Laud and Charles now faced more pressing problems than a small, determined outpost of dissent on the other side of the Atlantic, and before long, they both would be beheaded by the puritan-led English parliament. The colony was safe from Vane (or anyone else) coming as governor-general, although pessimists like Shepard would still be worrying for another year or two. Through luck and determination, the rulers of Massachusetts had weathered a potentially fatal storm, in large measure of their own making. It would be another half century before the Massachusetts Bay Colony's charter was permanently voided.

In Boston itself, Hutchinson's departure left behind large eddies of disturbance. Those men in the congregation present in Massachusetts may have agreed to excommunicate her. But women had no vote or voice there, and a few subsequently expressed their dissatisfaction with the trial loudly enough to provoke official reaction. The church excommunicated Edward Hutchinson's maidservant, Judith Smith, within a month of Hutchinson for public and private persistence in errors and for "sundry lyes then expressed by her and persisted in." Robert Harding and his wife, Philip, were extremely vocal in their criticisms, and the General Court ordered them to confer with Cotton and Wilson. Robert Harding made submission to Wilson, which satisfied the Court, but his wife did not, asserting in the Court that Hutchinson had deserved neither civil nor church censure. The Court handed her over to the Boston church, which excommunicated her "as a slanderer and reviler both of the Church and commonwealth." Thereupon she went off to Aquidneck on her own (her husband followed later). Mary Dyer seems to have been excommunicated, although the church records make no mention of it. Eventually the church excommunicated two males, John Underhill in 1640 and Anne Hutchinson's son Francis in 1641. Underhill mixed adultery with defiance about the Wheelwright petition; Francis Hutchinson was brazenly abusive on a visit back from Aquidneck, but he had been asking the church in vain to be released from his membership.

Dyer, Harding, and Smith give credence to the authorities' concern about Hutchinson's appeal to her own sex, but how many women these critics spoke for is unknown. Winthrop said that several women, appalled at Hutchinson's trial by her insistence that she had never denied sanctification, wanted to offer their own testimony to the contrary, but their "modesty" prevented them. The gender difference between the Boston and Roxbury excommunications, three or four women and eventually two men against five or six men, is striking. It might reflect the more limited geographic range of the women's childbirth networks in which Hutchinson was at her most effective. It also may indicate that women were attracted to Hutchinson as much or more by her personal qualities as by what various scholars have theorized was the special appeal of her doctrines to women, an appeal they have explained in different ways. That possibility is supported by an anecdote related by Anne's descendant, Massachusetts governor Thomas Hutchinson. Anne's great-granddaughter told him that a very elderly woman who had been a servant of Anne's remembered her as "not only as a truly pious woman but as a kind benevolent woman forward in every good office." Doctrine was not an issue one way or the other in this ancient memory of a visible saint.

Actual number of female "Hutchinsonians," however, is not the key issue in the authorities' concern about Hutchinson's influence on women. Men revealed their affiliations with overt acts like signing the Wheelwright petition, for which they could then be disciplined. Women tended not to, as the difficulty of convicting Hutchinson demonstrated. The women's childbirth and other social networks were opaque to men, and the nature and extent of Hutchinson's impact in them did not lend themselves to easy male assessment.

We do not know, for example, which radical it was whom Elizabeth

Wilson brought to her husband, John, near the end of 1636 for a frank talk about theology. All we know is that the talk pushed Elizabeth's alarmed husband into his pulpit opposition. Elizabeth probably gave verbal agreement to John as he explained to her how dangerous the radical's ideas were. Yet John knew that his wife was independent minded — she had resisted his attempts to get her to join him in Massachusetts for five years, while in 1649, hers was the first signature on a women's petition to the General Court on behalf of a midwife convicted of malpractice. As the free grace controversy raged, John must have at least occasionally wondered and worried while his wife went off for another protracted stint of helping at a childbirth. The town midwife, Jane Hawkins, was an overt follower of Hutchinson's. Hutchinson herself might show up. Who knew what would be discussed, and who knew how firmly Elizabeth really accepted that obeying Christ and obeying her husband were harmonious obligations? And what might result once a woman did start listening seriously to Hutchinson? It was said that the magistrate Richard Dummer was converted to Boston opinions through his wife.

Perhaps 1636–37 was a period when Boston women felt unusually free, or unusually impelled, to voice questions and opinions, even if they did not necessarily agree with Hutchinson. Wheelwright, in his fast-day sermon, called on the "men of Israel" to "fight for Christ," and two of the three "men" of ancient Israel he cited as examples were female heroes (Deborah and Jael). The recorded male uneasiness about Hutchinson's destabilizing effect on women never approached the anxiety expressed over crazed, gun-toting males, nor over Vane returning to institute tyranny, nor over the intrinsic lethality of the familist doctrines, real or imagined, in circulation, but it added to the concern among the authorities about Boston's hidden mysteries.

Yet the more these mysteries were exposed, the faster they evaporated. Winthrop and Weld both claimed that Hutchinson's defense of heresies at her church trial and her apparent lying opened the eyes of a number of her admirers and caused a significant drop in the esteem she enjoyed. Another event at the trial hastened lay disengagement from the radicals. As Mary Dyer rose and followed Hutchinson out of the church, someone remarked that she had delivered a dead fetus the previous fall, a "monstrous" birth, as these were called at the time. That comment made her previously concealed birth public knowledge. The following September, Hutchinson herself delivered a badly deformed stillborn fetus in Aquidneck. In England the laity commonly interpreted monstrous births as divine punishments for the moral lapses of their parents, while the clergy drew broader and more public lessons from them. For Dyer's and Hutchinson's births, both readings fused. The standard orthodox interpretation was that God sent the monsters as punishment and as a commentary on Hutchinson's monstrous opinions. According to Weld, the births, when added to the open heretical opinions and loosening of puritan strictness, had an especially strong effect on the radicals' admirers. They "dared not sleight so manifest a signe from Heaven" — if you were beginning to wonder if Hutchinson and her circle were truly among the godly, the monsters seemed to speak decisively to the question.

While the laity started to disengage from the theological radicals, the Boston elders pursued a course of moderation. As Cotton worked his way back to respectability, he toned down his preaching until it was almost indistinguishable from the other ministers'. His confrontational period over, he resumed his former preeminence, "like the clear shining of the sun after rain," as William Hubbard tactfully put it. He left some of his listeners, however, feeling stranded. Coddington wrote Cotton from Aquidneck in early 1641 that "it hath been reported to us that Mr. Cotton now holds forth things so darkly that if we had not known what he held forth before we knew not how to understand him."

On the other hand, both Cotton and Wilson seem to have treated erroneous opinions in their congregation very gently, since we know of only one person besides Hutchinson who was admonished for them. The Mount Wollaston community, with no resident preacher until late 1639, was a place in particular where errors were said to continue to thrive. But distant from Boston, and with no prominent members of the ministerial/magisterial elite to raise those errors to great heights, Mount Wollaston could be left alone. Cotton's congregation heard him preach in 1640 that "Godly women . . . may sometimes be more apprehensive [knowledgeable] of the mysteries of Salvation than the best ministers of the Gospel."

Cotton and Wilson also accepted the unrepentant Wheelwright in New Hampshire as a legitimate minister with a legitimate church. By contrast, as late as 1642, Weld and Eliot regarded Wheelwright's doctrine as heretical. Meanwhile, Cotton worked hard to come up with verbal fudging formulas whereby Wheelwright and others could come to terms with their opponents without ostensibly meaning anything different than they had all along. Wheelwright had his sentence of banishment lifted in 1644, after an extremely halfhearted apology to the General Court. Hutchinson, as will be seen below in this chapter, had no intention of apologizing to anyone.

The light touch of the church elders, along with lay disengagement from the extreme radicals and the departure of those who were irreconcilable, went a long way toward healing the divisions in the Boston church. At the end of 1639 Winthrop claimed that "all breaches were made up." He explained the preservation of the church as owing to Wilson and himself "carrying themselves lovingly and helpfully upon all occasions" and "not withdrawing themselves, (as they were strongly solicited to have done)."

What to the Boston church was the gentle restoration of the bonds of love, however, was to Thomas Shepard the avoidance of necessary, painful surgery. His opponents dared not defend their doctrines openly, but they had not reformed to Shepard's strict standards of intolerance: "Though they keep it in, yet how many are there whose hearts go after these detestable things!" They had worshiped a "new Calf," he lamented from the pulpit in 1639, and "never shall our glory be recovered till these evils are confessed and lamented, and the sin of the heart, which begat them." But with the chief agitators gone, the Boston church was untouchable. "Mr. Cotton repents not, but is hid," Shepard wrote grimly and impotently to himself early that year.

Shepard had reason to fret and fume, for the free grace controversy provoked few changes in Massachusetts. The General Court made the immigration order permanent. There is evidence that in the wake of the controversy, laity and ministers alike showed appreciation for the usefulness of conversion narratives in keeping doctrinal deviants out of the churches.

What the controversy did not do was lead to any adjustment to the institutions of Massachusetts's extraordinary quasi republic. For the rest of the seventeenth century, the colony continued to lumber along with its unlikely combination of representative government by the saints, uneasy separation of church and state, local congregational autonomy, and aggressive religious intolerance. It never again had to deal with a runaway church like Salem or Boston. Nonetheless, whenever Massachusetts churches seriously disagreed among themselves, as in the Half-Way Covenant dispute over baptism in the later 1660s, the lack of a higher ecclesiastical body with the power to compel obedience continued to mean that the results would shake both the churches and the state.

Where the free grace controversy did have a major impact was on the cultural geography of New England. The three most important ministers to come to America, Cotton, Hooker, and Davenport, each saw fit to reside in a separate colony. It has long been surmised that one of the reasons Hooker set up Connecticut was his desire to put distance between himself and Cotton. Ego and differing ideas on church government have been advanced as possible sources of tension. We now know that Hooker departed warning about Cotton's teaching on assurance. Davenport and his followers in the spring of 1638 gave their concern about a possible royal governor-general as one reason for leaving Massachusetts, and it cannot be a coincidence that in New Haven they set up a famously severe church and state disciplinary order that would have whipped a Hutchinson, Wheelwright, or Vane into line or out in very short order. "Wee were not worthy of Mr. Davenport and his People here," wrote Cotton upon their leaving Massachusetts. Wheelwright and his followers pushed puritanism into New Hampshire and then into Maine, territory previously associated with godless fishermen. Heterodox, semianarchic, and religiously tolerant Rhode Island managed to survive among its land-hungry and none too scrupulous neighbors due in no small measure to the accumulation of ability and population it acquired as fallout from the trials of Wheelwright and his associates. The differences that might have finished Massachusetts played a significant role in giving New England its eventual shape.

———

Exile launched Anne Hutchinson on a strange new journey of liberation. The popular image of her, banished from Massachusetts as a leader of dissent and/or a crusader for religious liberty and a protofeminist, has a complicated relationship to the truth of her life. Hutchinson in Massachusetts accepted that the saints were in an eternal life-or-death struggle with the preachers of false doctrine, whom she and her allies did their best to silence. There is no reason to think that she disagreed with Vane's claim that Massachusetts had the right to keep people with incorrect beliefs out of the colony. Far from being a feminist, Hutchinson defended herself at her civil trial by arguing that she had never violated the boundaries of women's place in society. She had never, she claimed, been a public actor and never uttered public speech; she confined her leadership activities to women. Hutchinson was an assertive woman and an adventurous religious thinker who by both hostile and sympathetic accounts enjoyed having admirers, but she worked effectively and satisfyingly behind the shelter offered by males like Cotton, Wheelwright, and Vane.

The new colony of Aquidneck had different de facto rules. Religious liberty, desired or not, was unavoidable. The followers of Wheelwright were appalled at the heretics among whom they found themselves. Wheelwright himself refused to move to the colony for that reason (he would eventually sanction the whipping of Quakers in New Hampshire). There was no way, however, that the more conservative exiles could impose their version of orthodoxy on the radicals. While scholarly and popular accounts of Hutchinson often assume that she dominated and sometimes that she even founded Aquidneck, she was hardly in a position to do so. The freedom of the new colony did not even result among the radicals in the dominance of "Hutchinsonians"; rather, it led to a profusion of prophets. In December 1638, Winthrop wrote with grim satisfaction about new errors being voiced by new would-be theologians there; Nicholas Easton, from Newbury, outdid Hutchinson in denigrating sanctification. One Herne, an obscure figure, taught that women had no souls. Samuel Gorton, an aggressive sect master heavily influenced by familism, soon settled nearby and attracted some of the exiles. If Hutchinson wanted influence in this free-for-all, she would have to fend for herself and assert a public voice.

Which is what she did. She set up meetings at her house on Sundays and now taught both men and women together. An earthquake struck New England on June 1, 1638, while Hutchinson and her followers were at prayer. According to Winthrop, they interpreted the earthquake as the descent of the Holy Spirit upon them. With the blessing of God clearly so behind her, Hutchinson engaged in what amounted to a guerrilla holy war against the Boston church. She wrote the congregation and the elders admonitions and predictions of the doom of Massachusetts and its churches. The Boston church sent a delegation to Aquidneck in 1640 that tried to convince Hutchinson of her errors and restore her to the church. Hutchinson, however, had no interest in repentance. She told them that their church was not a church of Christ. William Hutchinson said that he was "more nearly tied to his wife than to the church."

Not only did Hutchinson find a public voice in Aquidneck, after having to accept religious liberty as a fact of life, she eventually committed herself to it on principle. Around 1640 Hutchinson and her three or four families of followers became Seekers. Seekers were not a sect but holders of a disillusioned outlook on the state of Christianity that had circulated at the very fringes of the most radical puritan circles for half a century. Seekers rejected the puritan effort to create reformed churches. They believed that there had been no true churches in the world since the time of Jesus' apostles and there could be no true churches until God sent new apostles to found them. Since all churches were false, the government could not favor one church or punish others. The most prominent English Seekers, the Legate brothers, had been anti-Trinitarians, for which they were burned at the stake in 1613. It may not be a coincidence that Hutchinson's circle seems to have started questioning traditional understandings of the Trinity itself (or become more open in expressing what would have been the most hidden and dangerous element in Boston lay theology).

As Hutchinson became more of a public figure and even more radical than in Boston, the attention of Massachusetts turned to Narragansett Bay. In the early 1640s, Massachusetts began attempting to annex land near Aquidneck and indicated that it wanted to gain control of the entire Narragansett Bay region. Roger Williams's alarm was such that he returned to England to seek a proper charter for the Narragansett Bay settlements (his effort would lead to the present state of Rhode Island). As the Massachusetts disciplinary juggernaut rolled closer, Hutchinson and her family feared jail or worse should Massachusetts take over their colony. Hutchinson's last recorded new scriptural revelation, after her husband died in 1642, was that the Lord had prepared a city of refuge for her in what is now the Bronx in New York City, then claimed by New Netherland.

Hutchinson's city of refuge lay in the midst of the Wecqueasgeek band of Indians, who were participants in the intermittent bloody clashes with the Dutch known as Governor Kieft's War (1640–45).

The Indians warned Hutchinson not to settle among them. But she remembered the scripture verses that had assured her of salvation and divine protection back in England and asserted that "though all nations and people were cut off round them, yet should not they." She and the Wecqueasgeek, she told them, were "all one Indian." Her assertion of shared identity is an eloquent and haunting terminal point of the long journey that this courageous Lincolnshire gentlewoman made to the geographic, social, and spiritual margins of her culture. On the other hand, Hutchinson had the confidence to reply to the Wecqueasgeek as she did because she knew that a warning from idol worshipers could not override a promise of protection from the Christian God. She was wrong, possibly because a corrupt Dutch official never passed on her payment for her land to the Wecqueasgeeks. In August or September 1643 the Indians killed her and most members of the three families with her. They then drove the settlers' cattle, hated symbols of English imperialism, into their houses and burned the houses down. Sixteen people died, according to Winthrop; a few women and children escaped by boat.

—————

Hutchinson's personal influence proved ephemeral. Most of her followers died with her in the Indian raid. In Rhode Island, radical theology such as Hutchinson expounded was largely sucked into the new, familist-inspired Quaker movement, which reached the colony from England in 1656. The Quakers rejected predestination, and there was thus for them no assurance of salvation through an absolute promise. Still, in their talk of an indwelling Christ and the revelations of the Spirit, the Massachusetts exiles would have heard much that was familiar from the days of the most glorious church in the world. The Quakers practiced a radical spiritual equality of the sexes, which might have seemed a logical extension of implicit trends in Boston in 1637. At least ten exiles, including the Wheelwright supporter Coddington and Hutchinson's two closest known followers, Mary Dyer and Jane Hawkins, identified with the Quakers.

Winthrop's deliberately semifictionalized Hutchinson, the revelation-driven leader of an anarchic faction who would have destroyed the churches and the government of Massachusetts, did have lasting impact. *A Short Story*, the official Massachusetts account of the free grace controversy, went through three London editions in 1644 and was republished in London in 1692 at the time of a similar controversy there. Cotton Mather shortly thereafter recycled Winthrop's version of Hutchinson in his *Magnalia Christi Americana*, which became a standard source for early New England history. Throughout the seventeenth century, defenders of an orthodox godly commonwealth on both sides of the Atlantic were fascinated by the extraordinary symmetry of God's justice in inflicting a monstrous birth on such an exemplar of monstrous soul-damning doctrine and monstrous socially destructive disorder as Hutchinson.

The godly commonwealth ideal lost some of its rigidity by the turn of the eighteenth century. After two centuries of bloody, inconclusive European religious conflict, it became more widely accepted that different paths to God were an unavoidable fact of life and that they did not necessarily need to concern the state. In Massachusetts, the tight but explosive overarching alliance of the state and the churches came to an end in 1692. A new royal charter made property, not church membership, the basis of the franchise and required that the governor be appointed by the crown. The rulers and magistrates of Massachusetts would not necessarily be godly anymore. Congregationalism remained the official state-supported denomination, but other groups could petition for their own churches. By the end of the eighteenth century, Calvinism itself came under sharp attack, even in the Congregational churches. Yet given Massachusetts's history, it is no accident that by the time Massachusetts finally disestablished the Congregationalists in 1833, it was the last state in the union to have a government-supported church. In a final gesture of the old disciplinary project, a few years later, Massachusetts became the last state to imprison someone for seditious blasphemy, Abner Kneeland, who had written a tract arguing that God and nature were identical.

Kneeland would have been executed in the seventeenth century; however, in the nineteenth, he became a culture hero, and his prosecutors laughingstocks. In this more liberal atmosphere, it was no longer self-evident that even a character as menacing as the Anne Hutchinson that Winthrop created genuinely threatened the state. And if she did, the general rejection of Calvinism as narrow and barbarously harsh procured her a great deal of sympathy as a heroic dissenter. That sympathy was only heightened by Thomas Hutchinson's printing of the anonymous notes of Hutchinson's civil trial in his history of Massachusetts in 1764. The changed cultural climate and expanded sources allowed historians to read values into and onto the Hutchinson of Winthrop's account that she never dreamed of herself. Those values were always progressive. They made Hutchinson representative of the upward movement of society out of an unenlightened and repressive past. Recent scholarship recasting the disputes in which she was enmeshed in terms of gender, with Hutchinson by definition still at their center, is a continuation of this progressive approach to her.

Thus, the Hutchinson who survives today is in significant measure a continually revised product not of Hutchinson herself but of Winthrop's artistry, prejudices, and immediate polemical needs. However, Winthrop's work of art obviously draws heavily on Hutchinson for its inspiration. It can do so precisely because puritanism provided Hutchinson with the materials to make of her own life a work of art: the prophet of liberation in the Last Days of the world, participating in the downfall of Antichrist and assisting her brethren and sisters to truth and salvation. The story of herself that she acted out was received appreciatively, to varying degrees, and in varying depths, by a wide audience, and it lent itself easily enough to the commanding character that Winthrop made of her.

Restored to her historical context in Massachusetts, Hutchinson is not so obviously a harbinger of a more enlightened time. Yet she and her most virulent opponents were collectively representative of an important moment in the prehistory of religious liberty. Their mutual intolerance stemmed from their sharing in what the English historian Patrick Collinson has called the characteristic puritan drive toward a "monolithic, disciplined, Christian community." The intense religious life of the puritans, however, with its antiauthoritarian undercurrents, served to undercut that drive. Puritan ministers demanded deference from the laity. But they encouraged them to check their sermons by the Bible, and they stressed that the consent of the "people" was fundamental to church and state. They expected women to remain subordinate while telling them that they should love Christ more than their husbands. While preaching a demanding, even grueling, piety, the ministers themselves sometimes clashed on critical points of doctrine, even as deeply heterodox opinions flourished on the fringes of the movement. Puritans maintained an uneasy, pick-and-choose relationship with the religious and secular laws of England, while the laity pursued their religious lives in unsupervised semilegal private gatherings. Ministers and laity alike kept up a vociferous and sometimes savage stream of criticism directed at more conservative ministers in the Church of England. It was inevitable that this movement for a monolithic, disciplined community would attract and foster a wide diversity of opinionated men and women, whose deference to human authority was erratic at best.

In England, the tension between intolerance and diversity resulted in religious chaos when puritans took power in the 1640s, after eighty years as a loose movement of piety, protest, and reform. Whippings and imprisonments failed to stem a flood of Protestant radical sects. That failure came in part because more conservative puritans were unable to agree on a new form of national church government, due to irreconcilable, bitter differences between the presbyterian majority and a small group of New England–inspired congregationalists. Frightened by this confusion, the English people welcomed the end of the experiment in puritan government and the return of Charles I's son, Charles II, in 1660. English puritans would never again be in a position to implement a godly commonwealth.

American puritans avoided the full disruptive consequences of puritanism's inflammable mixture of intolerance and diversity because of New England's special circumstances. The General Court could ship Hutchinson and her prophetic powers off to an obscure corner of the region. Vane, by leaving, gave the Massachusetts establishment a chance to reconstitute and reassert itself, while others seriously unhappy with the turn of events in the colony did not need to stay around to defend a lost cause. Massachusetts's magistrates did not need to take seriously Wheelwright's suggestion that they execute him.

As with many other religious disputes of the founding years of New England, mobility ultimately defused the free grace controversy. That suggests that the single most important underlying factor in the successful institutionalization of puritanism in New England was the initial decimation of the Indians through epidemics and war. A reduced native population greatly facilitated the process of visible saints moving away from each other. The puritan zealotry that repeatedly flared up so dangerously thereby bought time to cool down into something less flammable and leave America with its long-enduring legacy of high intellectual endeavor, communitarianism, visionary zeal, and coercive, moralistic evangelism.

But not everyone seized with an unconventional, nonnegotiable religious impulse was prepared to move. In New England, as well as England, the capacity of godly dissenters to endure legal repression often exceeded the willingness of the magistrates to inflict suffering on people who were obviously devout Protestants of strong convictions. By the 1670s, Baptists and Quakers, after whippings, banishments, and even hangings, had established precarious and technically illegal toeholds in Massachusetts simply because public opinion limited the harshness with which the magistrates could pursue them. The very intensity of the intolerance with which Hutchinson and her opponents treated each other was an important step in Hutchinson's own forced discovery of religious tolerance, or rather of the futility of religious oppression. It is also representative of an intense period of unresolvable conflict among English Protestants that eventually and unintentionally led to toleration becoming official government policy on both sides of the Atlantic.

———

Religious diversity is a given today, but the historical Hutchinson is also representative of religious impulses that are far from played out in America. Evangelical Christians are still divided between those who give their primary allegiance to the word of the Bible and those who seek the Spirit behind it. The misunderstandings and mutual mistrust between the two groups have a faint but perceptible resonance with the conflicts that wracked Massachusetts in the 1630s.

Puritanism's ideal of the mutual reinforcement of religion and the state remains alive, as recent controversial efforts by the Bush administration to strengthen ties between the churches and the national government demonstrate. Both Hutchinson and her opponents in their Massachusetts fight would have fully appreciated Reverend Jerry Falwell's analysis of the tragedy of 9/11 as a divine response to a nation that had strayed from God's path through tolerance of pagans, abortionists, feminists, and gays. They would have heartily agreed with Christian Coalition founder Pat Robertson's warning about the satanic forces at play in politics and with his call for godly leaders. They might very well have broadly sympathized with the strident support among many evangelicals for an expansionist Israeli state in preparation for the Jews' conversion to Christianity and the glorious millennial church.

There are even some people for whom early Massachusetts itself is not a distant and outdated moment in history. The Christian Reconstructionists, who have had a significant influence on the evangelical political right, look upon the colony, with its death penalty for adulterers and disobedient children, subordination of women, and restriction of the franchise to church members, as a model to strive to re-create, with stealth, patience, and prayers. Only a storm of protest prevented President George Bush Jr. from appointing a Christian Reconstructionist as head of the National Labor Relations Board. The Christian Reconstructionists have one major innovation on the Massachusetts General Court. Should their back-to-the-future aspirations for American society come true, an account of the trials of a future Anne Hutchinson might end with a future Shepard having the opportunity to literally cast the first stone at her execution.

CHRONOLOGY

1591	Anne Marbury Hutchinson born; presbyterian movement suppressed.
1603	Elizabeth dies; James IV of Scotland assumes throne of England as James I.
1604	James I dashes puritan hopes for further reform of the Church of England.
1625	James I dies; his son becomes Charles I.
1627	Charles I exacts a "Forced Loan" from his subjects; planning for Massachusetts Bay Colony begins.
1629	Massachusetts Bay Company receives royal charter; Charles dissolves parliament, will not call another one until 1640.
1630	Beginning of Great Migration to Massachusetts.
1633	William Laud made archbishop of Canterbury; John Cotton arrives in Boston.
1634	The reconstituted General Court of the Massachusetts Bay Company becomes the legislative and chief judicial body in Massachusetts; Anne Hutchinson arrives in Boston.
1635	Thomas Shepard, John Wheelwright, John Wilson, and Henry Vane arrive in the colony; Roger Williams banished.
Spring 1636	Vane elected governor; exchange of letters between Cotton and Shepard.
October 1636	Conference between Cotton, Hutchinson, Wheelwright, and ministers; Winthrop blocks Wheelwright's appointment as coteacher of Boston church.
December 1636	General Court calls for fast day.
January 1637	Ministers' pulpit attacks on their opponents escalate; Wheelwright preaches fast-day sermon.
March 1637	Trial of Wheelwright in the General Court and subsequent protests.
May 1637	Winthrop elected governor; Massachusetts Bay Company charter revoked.

Summer 1637	Planned emigration of Cotton, Vane, and others falls through; Vane leaves for England; synod of New England churches; Scotland revolts against King Charles.
November 1637	Trials of supporters of Wheelwright in General Court; Hutchinson and two others banished.
March 1638	Boston church tries and excommunicates Hutchinson; Hutchinson and others go to Narragansett Bay.
1642	Hutchinson and followers move to present-day Bronx; war breaks out between King Charles I and puritan-led Parliament.
1643	Vane plays major role in negotiating the Solemn League and Covenant between parliament and the Scottish rebels; Hutchinson and most of immediate family killed in Indian raid.

Antichrist. Next to Satan, the greatest adversary of Christ, but masquerades as Christ's most fervent supporter. Puritans assumed that the pope was Antichrist, but they believed that Antichrist's influence pervaded the Church of England.

antinomianism. The belief that those whom God has saved are freed from the commanding power of his Laws. They obey God purely out of love, not out of duty or fear of punishment. Most puritans considered antinomianism simply an excuse for ceasing to struggle against sin.

covenant of grace. The agreement God made for the salvation of the elect (whether the agreement was with Jesus or the elect or in some way with both was a matter of debate). Jesus on the cross took the guilt and punishment that the sins of the elect deserve. Because of Christ's sacrifice, the elect go to heaven.

covenant of works. An agreement made between God and the first man, Adam. As long as Adam (and Eve) continued to perfectly obey God's will, God promised that they and all their posterity would continue in perfect happiness. The covenant of works is still in effect, but no one can fulfill its terms because everyone is born with original sin stemming from Adam and Eve's disobedience to God.

the elect. Those humans and angels whom God predestined to go to heaven.

faith. The acceptance of Christ as one's savior. Faith, if genuine, puritans insisted, is purely a gift of God, given by virtue of the covenant of grace.

familism. The Family of Love began in the sixteenth century in Germany. Familists believed that Christians under the illumination of the Holy Spirit could eventually enjoy perfect union with God and freedom from both sin and the responsibility for it. They believed that their own revelations superseded the Bible. Many of their ideas went back to the murderous, revelation-driven radical Protestant anabaptists of Münster, Germany, in the 1530s. In England, Familism underwent many, mostly unrecorded, grassroots mutations and adaptations.

grace. The freely bestowed favor and goodwill of God.

justification. God's pardon of the elect for their original and actual sin and His acceptance of Christ's perfect righteousness in place of their own sinful nature. Almost all puritans considered justification to take place during the lifetime of the elect.

predestination. God, before creating the universe, unalterably decreed that some particular men and angels would go to heaven and others would go to hell. As the puritan Westminster Confession of Faith (1646) puts it, "These angels and men, thus predestinated and foreordained, are particularly and unchangeably designed; and their number is so certain and definite that it cannot be either increased or diminished."

sanctification. The creation of a new holiness in believers that follows justification. While people who have not been justified can follow God's laws, puritans called such behavior legal obedience because it did not come out of true holiness. Whether it was possible to distinguish righteous behavior that came from sanctification (which meant that one had been justified) and righteous behavior that came from legal obedience was one of the hottest areas of dispute between Cotton and the other ministers.

witness (immediate), or Seal of the Spirit. A direct communication from the Holy Spirit to believers that God has saved them through a scripture verse like "I am thy salvation." Many puritan ministers denied the reality of this communication. John Cotton was the only prominent puritan minister who not only accepted it but insisted that it was the primary and first vehicle of assurance of salvation.

BIBLIOGRAPHIC ESSAY

Note from the series editors: The following bibliographical essay will lead readers to the primary and secondary sources the author consulted for this volume. We have asked all authors in the series to omit formal citations in order to make our volume more readable, inexpensive, and appealing for students and general readers.

Most of the substance of this book is derived from Michael P. Winship, *Making Heretics: Militant Protestantism and Free Grace in Massachusetts, 1636–1641* (Princeton, N.J., 2002). *Making Heretics* is the first major reexamination of the narrative of the free grace controversy in more than forty years, and it problematizes many of the conventional assumptions of the secondary literature. Readers should refer to *Making Heretics* for extended discussions of the reasons and documentation behind the interpretations in *The Times and Trials of Anne Hutchinson.* The text and endnotes of *Making Heretics* discuss at length the extensive relevant primary and secondary sources on Hutchinson and on the controversies in which she was involved.

For a lengthy, detailed, and imaginatively (sometimes very imaginatively) written account of Hutchinson and the free grace controversy, see Emery Battis, *Saints and Sectaries: Anne Hutchinson and the Antinomian Controversy in the Massachusetts Bay Colony* (Chapel Hill, N.C., 1962). Battis has much valuable information, but his book's central thesis, that Hutchinson suffered from the twin curses of menopause and a weak husband, has been largely ignored, except to be held up for either indignation or ridicule. Battis, *Saints and Sectaries*, Darren Staloff, *The Making of an American Thinking Class: Intellectuals and Intelligentsia in Puritan Massachusetts* (New York, 1998), and Louise A. Breen, *Transgressing the Bounds: Subversive Enterprises among the Puritan Elite* (New York, 2001), are the main promulgators of the economic interpretations of Hutchinson and her allies discussed on p. 76.

Interpretations of the free grace controversy that emphasize Hutchinson usually emphasize gender. For pioneering and/or prominent examples of an extensive and diverse literature, see Ben Barker-Benfield, "Anne Hutchinson and the Puritan Attitude to Women," *Feminist Studies* 1 (1973): 65–96; Lyle Koehler, "The Case of the American Jezebels: Anne Hutchinson and Female Agitation during the Years of the Antinomian Turmoil, 1636–1640," *William and Mary Quarterly*, 3rd ser., 31 (1974): 55–78; Elaine Huber, *Women and the Authority of Inspiration* (Lanham, Md., 1987); Amy Schrager Lang, *Prophetic Woman: Anne Hutchinson and the Problem of Dissent in New England Literature* (Berkeley, 1987); Marilyn J. Westerkamp, "Anne Hutchinson, Sectarian Mysticism, and the Puritan Order," *Church History* 59 (1990): 482–96; Jane Kamensky, *Governing the Tongue: The Politics of Speech in Early New England* (New York,

1997); Amanda Porterfield, *Female Piety in New England: The Emergence of Religious Humanism* (New York, 1992); and Mary Beth Norton, *Founding Mothers and Fathers: Gendered Power and the Forming of American Society* (New York, 1996). Some of this literature is little more than polemic; some of it has valuable insights (I found the last two books cited here especially helpful). All of it takes as a given that Hutchinson was the central figure of the controversy. As a consequence, Vane and Wheelwright are labeled her "supporters" and "followers" and then largely ignored; Cotton goes mostly unexamined; and the multifaceted and multidirectional heresy hunting of men like Shepard is overlooked altogether.

The biographies of Anne Hutchinson are all popular rather than scholarly. They can be engaged and insightful but also underresearched, unreliable with facts, and hasty in interpretation. For the most recent example of the genre, with its vices and virtues, see Eve LaPlante, *American Jezebel : The Uncommon Life of Anne Hutchinson, the Woman Who Defied the Puritans* (San Francisco, 2004). For introductions to Hutchinson's piety, see James Fulton Maclear, " 'The Heart of New England Rent': The Mystical Element in Early Puritan History," *Mississippi Valley Historical Review* 42 (1956): 641–43; and Michael G. Ditmore, "A Prophetess in Her Own Country: An Exegesis of Anne Hutchinson's 'Immediate Revelations,' " *William and Mary Quarterly*, 3rd ser., 57 (2000): 349–92. See Lang, *Prophetic Woman*, for Hutchinson's historical image.

Hutchinson's trial before the General Court has acquired a lengthy literature, much of it anachronistic in its assumptions about justice and legal procedures. For a good appraisal of the legal charges against Hutchinson and her allies, see Battis, *Saints and Sectaries*, 212–22. For an analysis of the role gender assumptions played in both of Hutchinson's trials, see Norton, *Founding Mothers*, chap. 8. Most analyses of Hutchinson's conviction by the General Court do not find any legal justification for it. Some scholars present the trial as a sham from the start. See, for example, Kai T. Erikson, *Wayward Puritans: A Study in the Sociology of Deviance* (New York, 1996), 93, 94; and Ann Fairfax Withington and Jack Schwartz, "The Political Trial of Anne Hutchinson," *New England Quarterly* 51 (1978): 226–40. Another larger group claims that the legal basis for convicting Hutchinson collapsed when Cotton failed to remember damaging words from her. See, for example, Charles Francis Adams, *Three Episodes of Massachusetts History* (Boston, 1892), 1:499; Edmund S. Morgan, "The Case against Anne Hutchinson," *New England Quarterly* 10 (1937): 635–49; and Norton, *Founding Mothers*, 386. But Cotton acknowledged at Hutchinson's trial that his memory was incomplete. I see no evidence from the transcript that he was making a great impression on the court, nor any reason why he should have.

There is little in the much more limited literature on Hutchinson's church trial that is of much use, perhaps because scholars tend to skirt around the recondite theological debates that are at its core. Historians have not paid much attention to Wheelwright's trial, and when they have, they have relied on Winthrop's one-sided accounts.

The other main characters in the free grace controversy have received biographical attention of varying thoroughness. For Winthrop, see Edmund S. Morgan, *The Puritan Dilemma: The Story of John Winthrop*, rev. ed. (New York, 1998) and Francis J. Bremer, *John Winthrop: America's Forgotten Founding Father* (New York, 2003). For Cotton, see Larzer Ziff, *The Career of John Cotton: Puritanism and the American Experience* (Princeton, N.J., 1962). The best introduction to Wheelwright is Charles H. Bell, ed., *John Wheelwright*, Prince Society Publications 9 (Boston, 1872). For an introduction to Shepard, see Michael McGiffert, ed., *God's Plot: The Paradoxes of Puritan Piety, Being the Autobiography and Journal of Thomas Shepard* (Amherst, Mass., 1972). For Vane, see Violet A. Rowe, *Sir Henry Vane the Younger: A Study in Political and Administrative History* (London, 1970).

The single most influential twentieth-century article on the free grace controversy is Perry Miller, "'Preparation for Salvation' in Seventeenth-Century New England," *Journal of the History of Ideas* 4 (1943): 253–86. Miller's interpretation stresses two alleged dichotomies: the new civic-mindedness of the New England puritans versus the anarchic individualism of Cotton and Hutchinson; and the emphasis on preparation for grace by the orthodox ministers versus an emphasis on its spontaneous acceptance by Cotton and Hutchinson, with Cotton and Hutchinson thereby maintaining a more pristine spirituality than the ministers. Miller is wrong or at best heavily misleading on both counts. However, he is worth reading for the enormous and mostly unfortunate influence he has had on much of the subsequent scholarly discussion of the theology of the controversy, sometimes at one or two removes. See, for example, Norman Pettit, *The Heart Prepared: Grace and Conversion in Puritan Spiritual Life*, 2nd ed. (Middletown, Conn., 1989); Harry S. Stout, *The New England Soul: Preaching and Religious Culture in Colonial New England* (New York, 1986); Andrew Delbanco, *The Puritan Ordeal* (Cambridge, Mass., 1989); and Janice Knight, *Orthodoxies in Massachusetts: Rereading American Puritanism* (Cambridge, Mass., 1994), along with titles cited previously.

For detailed and careful studies of the areas of theological disagreement between Cotton and the other ministers, see William K. B. Stoever, *"A Faire and Easie Way to Heaven": Covenant Theology and Antinomianism in Early Massachusetts* (Middletown, Conn., 1978); and Theodore Dwight Bozeman, *The Precisianist Strain: Disciplinary Religion and Antinomian Backlash in Puritanism to 1638* (Chapel Hill, N.C., 2004). For an introduction to Henry Vane's theology, see David Parnham, *Sir Henry Vane, Theologian: A Study in Seventeenth-Century Religious and Political Discourse* (Madison, N.J., 1997). Parnham makes Vane's reliance on Cotton clear. For the influence of Boston radicalism on Vane, see my *Making Heretics*.

Stephen Foster, *The Long Argument: English Puritanism and the Shaping of New England Culture, 1570–1700* (Chapel Hill, N.C., 1991), provides a good synthetic account of puritanism from its sixteenth-century English origins to eighteenth-century New England. On New England congregationalism and its origins, see Edmund S. Morgan, *Visible Saints: The History of a Puritan Idea* (New York, 1963); David D. Hall, *The Faithful Shepherd: A History of the New England Ministry in the Seventeenth Century* (Chapel Hill, N.C., 1972); and James F. Cooper Jr., *Tenacious of Their Liberties: The Congregationalists in Colonial Massachusetts* (New York, 1999). For the puritan conversion experience, see Charles Lloyd Cohen, *God's Caress: The Psychology of Puritan Religious Experience* (New York, 1986). On the varieties of religious radicalism in early New England, see Philip F. Gura, *A Glimpse of Sion's Glory: Puritan Radicalism in New England, 1620–1660* (Middletown, Conn., 1984). For women and early Massachusetts puritanism, see Porterfield, *Female Piety*; and Marilyn J. Westerkamp, *Women and Religion in Early America, 1600–1850: The Puritan and Evangelical Traditions* (New York, 1999), chap. 2. On the process of immigration, see David Cressy, *Coming Over: Migration and Communication between England and New England in the Seventeenth Century* (New York, 1987).

For sixteenth-century English puritanism, Patrick Collinson, *The Elizabethan Puritan Movement* (Oxford, 1990), although originally published in 1968, remains the critical starting point. There is no similar defining volume for the early seventeenth century, but Peter Lake, *The Boxmaker's Revenge: "Orthodoxy," "Heterodoxy" and the Politics of the Parish in Early Stuart London* (Manchester, Eng., 2001), provides a good introduction. David R. Como, *Blown by the Spirit: Puritanism and the Emergence of an Antinomian Underground in Pre-Civil-War England* (Stanford, Calif., 2004), is a pathbreaking account of the antinomian/familist puritan subculture. Tom Webster, *Godly Clergy in Early Stuart England: The Caroline Puritan Movement c. 1620–1643* (Cambridge, Eng., 1997), has much to say on the region from which many New England ministers came and on the pressures that drove them to New England. On the English Dorchester puritan social experiment, see David D. Underdown, *Fire from Heaven: Life in an English Town in the Seventeenth Century* (New Haven, Conn., 1992).

For law and puritanism in early Massachusetts in general, I relied on George L. Haskins, *Law and Authority in Early Massachusetts: A Study in Tradition and Design* (New York, 1960); and John M. Murrin, "Magistrates, Sinners, and a Precarious Liberty: Trial by Jury in Seventeenth-Century New England," in *Saints and Revolutionaries: Essays in Early American History*, ed. David D. Hall, John M. Murrin, and Thad W. Tate (New York, 1984), 135–59. Also helpful is Barbara Black, "The Judicial Power and the General Court in Early Massachusetts" (Ph.D. diss., Yale University, 1975). For speech crimes in early British North America, see Larry D. Eldridge, *A Distant Her-*

itage: The Growth of Free Speech in Early America (New York, 1994); and Norton, *Founding Mothers*, chaps. 4 and 5. See Kamensky, *Governing the Tongue*, on speech in Massachusetts in general.

For easily accessible sets of primary sources on the free grace controversy, see David D. Hall, ed., *The Antinomian Controversy, 1636–1638: A Documentary History*, 2nd ed. (Durham, N.C., 1990); Richard S. Dunn, James Savage, and Laetitia Yeandle, eds., *The Journal of John Winthrop* (Cambridge, Mass., 1996); Allyn B. Forbes et al., eds., *The Winthrop Papers*, 5 vols. (Boston, 1929–47); and Sargent Bush Jr., ed., *The Correspondence of John Cotton, 1621–1652* (Chapel Hill, N.C., 2001).